THE
CHURCH
FROM CONCEPTION
TO MISCONCEPTION

How America's Church
Arrived in the Post Christian Era

BUCK L. KEELY

To my wife Susan, who has been my friend, encourager, and when necessary my critic that God has used to keep me on His course for my life.

It is true, "*Who can find a virtuous woman? for her price is far above rubies,*" and I have been blessed with finding this virtuous woman.

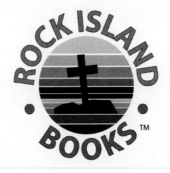

www.rockislandbooks.com

Visit our website to purchase books and
preview upcoming titles.

Contact us at:
feedback@rockislandbooks.com

Contents

Contents

Foreward

There was a time over a 100 years ago when the deacons patrolled the aisles of the church with a switch, looking for anyone that was nodding off or had fallen asleep during the sermon. The offender, be he mayor or muckraker, was given a swift sharp switch to the back of the head and immediately they were awakened and at full attention.

In churches today, if you are awake and alert, asking questions about the whys and wherefores of the modern church, you find yourself encouraged to go back to sleep. In some cases you will be invited to leave, as your agitation is surely going to disturb the restful sleep of others.

Buck Keely has written a book that is a switch to the back of the head of the sleepy, groggy, institutional church. His book is skillfully written, extremely well researched, and clearly meant to retrace the "By-Path Meadow," trailing back though all the deception and double talk that is now the "Blabber Speak" of the modern institutional church, in order that you might be encouraged to return to the roots that give life to the branches. Buck answers the question that many are now asking, "How did the church come to be in its current sorry state?" Buck Keely offers a biblical template that is not just ideal, but was once the norm of the true pilgrim church that Christ inaugurated after His resurrection.

You will find this book both deeply disturbing and greatly encouraging. Buck Keely is not a "theoreticalist" but a man of keen insight with decades of experience as a church planter and pastor. Buck is an evangelist whose heart groans at the sorry condition of a Church that has gone terribly wrong and is putting so many souls at peril.

I have known Buck Keely for many years and have spent hours of fruitful discussions regarding the spiritual condition of the institutional church. The first things I learned about Buck was that he had a mind that worked like a steel trap, a knowledge of the Scriptures that was truly exhaustive, and a broken heart for the modern day institutional "evangelical" church. A rare combination of mental steel and spiritual insight that is keen to tear away the façade of religiosity so that sinners might see, love, and follow the Savior.

As the founder of Rock Island Books, a Christian publishing house, I am dedicated to the building up of the brethren in Christ. I am very proud to be publishing a book that is both a history and a battle cry to return to our Savior, and a call to conduct ourselves in our assembly in a way that is informed by the Scriptures and given life by the Spirit of God. Buck is calling us to abandon the fake, ever changing and capricious traditions and politics of men, and humbly return to the only one who can give us life and hope.

I invite you to read this book, written by the modern version of "Great Heart" the character in Bunyan's Pilgrims Progress that leads Christian to the Celestial City.

This is a book that should be on the library shelf of every bible-believing Christian. I have no doubt that the impact of this book on those that take the time to read it with a heart full of faith and an eye on the Scriptures alone, will be transforming.

-C.J. Lovik

Preface

This book has been forty years in the making. A pilgrimage starting as doubter and skeptic of God and His Church, to a follower and servant of the founder of the Church, and now an honest critic of the methods and practices of the Church. It is this relationship with the Lord's Church that drove me to the conclusion there are two distinct and separate relationships a person has with the Church. Most Christians will agree when a person is born again by God's Spirit they are joined with all the "Followers of the Way" in a spiritual relationship with the Triune God. What happens after this new beginning with Jesus as a part of His Bride, is where things get fuzzy and uncertain.

A journey back in time exploring the past 2000 plus years of church history will reveal the development of an alter-ego from the first born church in Jerusalem to the local church assemblies of today in America. This alter-ego develops around the born again who gather in local assemblies, and extends to denominational identities. The second identity a believer has with the church is constructed around the place and the people where assembled believers establish a local church. Church creeds, doctrinal mandates, and many other ancillary items are contributors in the build out of this alter-ego.

Webster defines the word institution as "a place where an organization takes care of people for a usually long period of time; or a custom, practice, or law that is accepted and used by many people." There is no question the Body of Christ from the time it was empowered with the "cloves of fire" until today has had, and continues to have, institutions with which they identify. The institutions surrounding the Lord's Church has changed as the church has developed from the apostle's rule, and as well was established in different cultures over the centuries. Decrees, customs and practices throughout church history can be easily observed with a backwards look at the development of the church in the past centuries.

There is an identity and an accountability a believer holds, both to and with this institution. Often the alter ego of the Lord's Church becomes the "Christian" identity of the believer. Indeed, the consequences of this identity drives the Christian to refocus most of their energy and effort away from the Lord's Church hosted in the institution. Many are erroneously devoted to the alter ego and not the true Body of Christ.

It is having the capacity to separate the institution of church, which is co-joined to the Lord's Church, which will allow an honest examination of ourselves and our relationship with God and His Church. The unraveling of these two identities will allow for the criticism of this alter ego without casting dispersion on the followers of Jesus and His Church. Followers of Jesus are joined to the Lord's church by the action of the Holy Spirit, and the born again identify and assemble with other believers in this "institution" to worship and serve the Saviour who loves us.

It is the *institution* of the Church to which I will devote the criticism I have of the Church.

Introduction

The Lord's Church was not, and is not, at risk of failure. The promise made for its endurance by its founder was sealed with His Blood. Indeed, the gates of hell have been opened against His Church, but yet she still remains strong and unwavering.

What has been successfully attacked by Satan and his cohorts is the institution that grows around the Lord's Church to support the needs, work, administration and ministries of the local body of believers. These institutions have come and gone throughout the centuries and have had different degrees of success in assisting the Lord's Church in her execution of the great commission as given by her founder.

Without exception, all of the institutions of the churches have, over time, taken over the Lord's Church that dwells in the midst of the institutional structure. The larger the institutions grow in numbers and assets, the more significance that is placed on the promotion, success and sometimes survival of the institution of the church, always at the expense of the Lord's Church. The institutions of church establish the polity, requirements for membership, and conditions of affiliation to be numbered among the "church" group identified with each institution.

AMERICA REDEFINES THE CHURCH'S INSTITUTION

The American Church has had a unique experience in the history of the Lord's Church. When the American Colonies rejected England's command and control over their national affairs, they drafted the documents of America's freedom to include the removal of power from religious institutions to exercise institutional authority over the political and religious will of the of the people. This change in the political position held by the institutions of the churches would change the dynamics the churches in America would have in shaping the relationship of church and civil governments.

Supporters of the American political structure often refer to "American exceptionalism" to delineate the difference between the political structure of America and the rest of the world's governments. When asked about America's exceptionalism, President Obama responded, "I suspect that the Brits believe in British exceptionalism and the Greeks believe in Greek exceptionalism." In his response, he revealed more than his lack of knowledge of what makes America exceptional, he stated his ideology that Americans are no different from every other people group of the world.

America as a nation does not embrace a national approach to God. America's view on religion is simple, a relationship with God is a personal relationship that is independent of outside influences. God and a person's relationship with Him is not legitimized or enforced by civil authorities. With this understanding, America's exceptionalism is not based upon the citizen's thoughts or frame of mind about national pride, or lack thereof. What makes America exceptional is how our nation is unlike any other nation that exists, or has existed, in its understanding of the role of government in religious matters. Framing the place and power civil authorities can have in granting or limiting the free exercise of a relationship with God and our fellow citizens is what makes America exceptional.

America's governmental approach differs from all other nations because of this single concept: God is the possessor and granter of any and all privileges available to humanity, "all men are created equal, that they are endowed by their Creator with certain unalienable rights." The understanding is simple, governments do not grant "rights," God does.

The effect on the institution of the Lord's Church established by America's exceptionalism created a different political environment for the Lord's Church and her institution than had previously existed in the history of mankind. The outcome of the enumerated rights expressed in our constitution established the understanding that American's relationship with God and His church was outside the scope of power available to civil authorities. This understanding differs from any other government in the world. The limit of the civil authorities in exercising control over its citizens through religious institutions and ending the ability of religious institutions establishing and exercising political power was created with these words, "Congress shall make no law respecting an establishment of religion, or prohibiting the free exercise thereof," found in the First Amendment of the Constitution of the United States.

There is no question that the first amendment has been attacked by the foes of God and His Church, but still it stands as the power that makes America's Church experience unique and different from any other place or time in the history of the Lord's

Church. Undeniably, the church in America has been shaped by what has been identified as "American Exceptionalism."

Throughout history, religion has established a synergy with civil governments, the governments use religion as a tool to control people groups, to garner power to establish a ruling class and the religious institutions use the government to enforce their dominance over other religious groups, establish polity that is protected from the general population, and to gain power and wealth for the religious institutions.

It matters little which religion discussed in relationship with its institution, the outcome looks much the same. With Judaism, Jesus attacked the institution with charges of replacing God's laws with man's laws, taking advantage of the less fortunate in society, using their religion as a tool to gain wealth, power and prestige. These same charges can be brought against all of the world religions, including Christianity. The Roman Catholic Church—empowered by the synergy with Constantine— brought about one of the most vile, evil church institutions that ever existed. Millions upon millions of lives were lost establishing and defending the power of this civil and religious arrangement.

The founders of the American documents that established the freedoms of the American people set apart the relationship between government and religious institutions. This was enacted to protect the American people; not from God's influence in their lives, but rather the religious institutions that seek to control the population, and to gain power and wealth from their protected position granted by civil authorities.

The outcome of this separation of religious institutions and civil government caused the institutions of the church in America to find new and inventive ways to establish numerical and financial wealth, and to gain and grow political favor from the civil authorities. America was formed with Christian values but the civil and religious institutions were separate and unrelated in the exercise of power over civil matters for the religious institutions and over religious matters for the civil authorities.

For the past two and half centuries, the relationship the institutions of the Lord's Church in America has held in civil government has changed over and over. We now are embarking upon a new journey in the relationship of the church's institutions and its place in civil government.

THE POST CHRISTIAN ERA IN AMERICA

America is now moving into a "Post Christian Era" relationship with the institutions of Church and civil government. The institutions of the church are losing prominence and power in civil matters. Matters of morality and ethics have been stripped from religious views and reassigned to cultural imperatives. The Christian understandings on issues such as abortion, sexual purity and homosexuality as presented and proclaimed by church institutions have caused a decline in membership and attendance. These intrusions will continue to decline as the civil governments make laws that will forbid the promotion of the Biblical views held by religious institutions concerning matters of morality and ethics.

The founding fathers never intended to have a "wall" of separation between our civil government and the expression of faith in its citizens. In fact, the very opposite is true.

John Adams said, "Our constitution was made only for a moral and religious people. It is wholly inadequate for the government of any other." Is there any question remaining why America has moved into a post Christian Era, understanding that the nation has embraced the ideology of the "separation of church and state," as pursued by the social progressives?

Benjamin Franklin, who never would be considered a religious zealot said, "I have lived a long time, and the longer I live, the more convincing proofs I see of this truth—that God Governs in the affairs of men. And if a sparrow cannot fall to the ground without His notice, is it probable that an empire can rise without His aid?"

Alexander Hamilton said with regard to the constitution, "For my own part, I sincerely esteem it a system which without the finger of God, never could have been suggested and agreed upon by such a diversity of interests." He also declared on the topic of the importance of Christianity, "Let an association be formed to be denominated 'The Christian Constitutional Society,' its object to be first: The support of the Christian religion. Second: The support of the United States."

George Mason in his support of the constitution said, "The laws of nature are the laws of God, whose authority can be superseded by no power on earth."

Thomas Pane, in his book Common Sense records, "The cause of America is in a great measure the cause of all mankind. Where, say some, is the king of America? I'll tell you, friend, He reigns above."

The list of statements and the men espousing the importance of God and His Church would consume thousands of pages, in fact there are many hundreds of books that have been published on this one subject. It is astounding with so much documentation on the importance of God and His Church that America has moved into a post Christian Era. The question has to be asked, how have the social progressives been so successful in removing the fingerprints of the founding fathers from the creation of the constitution that guides America's future? The answer lies within the educational system of America's public schools.

The battle for the hearts and minds of America begins in the institutions of higher learning. Social progressives have invested fifty years taking over the educational systems of America. These institutions of higher learning have become factories that produces social progressive clones that become the leaders of the institutions of business, education, government and religion. The goal of the institutions is not to enlighten or educate but to replicate an ideology of social progressiveness. America is now reaping the harvest of the social progressives' investment. The institutions of remedial and higher education, business and government are not just infiltrated by the product of social progressiveness but are owned by them.

It is sad to observe and note that many of the religious institutions as well have been subdued by the social progressives. The social progressives have been so successful in their message that one recent survey found seventy percent of all Americans believe that many religions can lead to eternal life, including sixty-five percent of all self-identifying Christians. In this same survey, it was found that unbelievably fifty-six percent of all Evangelical Christians believe that there are many paths, other than faith in Christ, to God and eternal life.

Americans have been brainwashed into believing the greatest gift a parent can give to their children is a college education. When children are at the height of rebellion and subject to influence they are packed up and sent away to be "re-educated" into secular citizens. Without question the educational institutions have been taken over by social progressives insomuch that anyone holding traditional American values will not be allowed to teach or express these ideas without the loss of title and position.

Social progressives seek and have been successful for the most part in secularizing America's culture. Little will be studied by the youth of America about the founding fathers and their understanding of God and His place in governing the people of America.

The pages of the text books teaching the truth of how men of faith structured our nation's documents not to be void of God's influence but to limit man's influence over the things of God have been ripped out of the teaching of American History. In public schools across America, the future leaders of America are being taught a revisionist's history, as the founding fathers are framed as evil white men who took privilege over other people in the establishment of the guiding documents that formed our nation, and that Christianity was and is an evil influence in world history.

The institutions of the church are losing prominence and power in civil matters. Matters of morality and ethics have been stripped from religious views and reassigned to cultural imperatives. The Christian understandings on issues such as abortion, sexual purity and homosexuality as presented and proclaimed by church institutions have caused a decline in membership and attendance. These intrusions will continue to decline as the civil governments make laws that will forbid the promotion of the Biblical views held by religious institutions concerning matters of morality and ethics.

The majority of religious institutions that are successful in at-

tracting large gatherings and assets are avoiding biblical teachings on morality and are focusing on "positive" messages, commonly referred to as the "Prosperity Gospel." In the next few
years, America's relationship with the institutions of church will
be fundamentally changed to reflect the current values held by
the American population.

The Lord's Church will not be hindered as America changes,
she will still preach the Gospel, minister, teach, and disciple,
and will remain until the Lord comes to receive her. The Lord's
Church has been, is currently, and will be the target of Satan and
his minions. Persecution has come from civil governments as
well as the institutions of the church, from her birth until today.
There is no question persecution of Lord's Church is increasing,
and will accelerate as we move into this "Post Christian Era."

In the Heart of God ⟨1⟩

Colossians 1:26
*Even the mystery which hath been hid from ages and
from generations, but now is made manifest to his saints.*

The Church of God was conceived in the womb of
sin. It came as no surprise to God when Man failed
in the Garden. God had already put in motion a plan
that would interrupt the promised outcome of sin. Indeed, Adam and Eve were the first to earn the wage of sin, and
God's remedy for the sinners was to vicariously atone sin's wages
through the blood of an animal. The blood spilt by God, when
he provided the skins of animals for a covering for the sin-aware
couple in the garden, established the method that would be kept
by repentant sinners until the church came into fruition.

Jesus' death would be the final blood offering that would once
and for all time settle the sin debt of the world. This offering is the
reason the Church came into existence. The Church that would
be born out of Jesus' sacrifice would be the holding place of the

born again believers. It also will be God's empowered messenger of the hope for the sinner who is assigned to God's judgment and wrath—this hope is found only in the preaching of the Gospel.

THE WRATH OF GOD SATISFIED

It was not the blood of an animal, nor was it the seat of mercy in the temple made with the hands of men that satisfied God's wrath, for "Neither by the blood of goats and calves, but by his own blood had he entered in once into the holy place, having obtained eternal redemption for us." Just as God Himself provided a sacrifice for Abraham on Mount Moriah, He would provide this final lamb. This sacrifice would not be the son of a man, but the Son of God. When Jesus presented His blood in heaven, the sin debt was paid in full for all sinners who would receive this sacrifice. This offering of the blood of Jesus would end the blood sacrifices offered at the hands of sinners to atone for the sin of mankind. It is true, the scripture "...without the shedding of blood there is no remission" remains as operational today as it was when God implemented it in the garden. From the first sin in the garden experienced by Eve, until the last sinner confronts their sin in the name of Jesus, the blood of God's perfect Lamb is sufficient, as the old hymn says, "The blood of Jesus will never lose its power."

God was the first to practice the cleansing of the sinner with the blood of an animal and Able brought a blood sacrifice for a sin offering and God received it. This practice would continue as an atonement for the sinner until the last prophet declared, "Behold the Lamb of God that taketh away the sin of the world." God himself provided the last offering of blood.

God's plan to redeem fallen man would be the topic of the prophets for centuries. God's word makes this clear, "God, who at sundry times and in divers manners spake in time past unto the fathers by the prophets," and as well "Surely the Lord GOD will do nothing, but he revealeth his secret unto his servants the prophets." When a child is conceived in the womb of a mother it is not long before the woman is awakened to the secret that is forming in her womb, and soon becomes aware of the life that now lives in her body. It will be weeks before anyone else will see the change in her body, and many more months before the child is birthed. In the same way a child is conceived as a secret in the womb of a woman, the church was conceived in the heart of God long before it was manifested.

THE LORD'S CHURCH: A SECRET IN HEAVEN

The plan of God for His Church was not fully exposed and completed until Jesus demoted Himself to become lower than the Angels and be to born of a virgin. The intent of the Church was revealed when Jesus stood before the men in Nazareth and declared, "The Spirit of the Lord is upon me, because he hath anointed me to preach the Gospel to the poor; he hath sent me to heal the brokenhearted, to preach deliverance to the captives, and recovering of sight to the blind, to set at liberty them that are bruised, To preach the acceptable year of the Lord."

Jesus speaking to God's plan for the debt of sinners said, "I will utter things which have been kept secret from the foundation of the world." What was this secret Jesus was about to reveal? The payment for the wages of the sinner was to be paid in full by His own blood. This offering of blood from Jesus who knew no sin would pay the sin debt of the repentant sinner, and this was God's will from the foundation of the world. The plan of God for His church was not only a mystery to God's servants on earth, it was a mystery to the servants in heaven. The proclaiming of the Holy Spirit filled men and women who were expounding the Gospel of Jesus bewildered the angels who were observing this event, it is said that this was so incredible "the angels desire to look into."

In the thousands of years mankind practiced sin, the blood of animals was the method used to postpone God's wrath and preserve fallen humanity. The sacrifices made by sinful men on behalf of men who had sinned would be repeated year after year until the perfect sacrifice would be made.

THE CHURCH OF GOD

Jesus' death on the cross was not simply the *final* payment; it was the *only* payment for sin. The sacrifices of the blood of animals were to be a reminder of the wages earned by the sinner and the wrath of God to be exercised on the unrepentant sinner. When Jesus payed the debt of sin for the sinners, it was finished. The sin debt for the world was paid in full, the sins of all who lived before Jesus' sacrifice, the sins of all who lived in the time Jesus walked on the earth, and all who would live after Jesus' death. Sin's ledger of debt was retired when Jesus was suspended between heaven and earth and died on Calvary's Hill. The church was the outcome of God's mercy and grace given to repentant sinners who are added to the body of faith by God Himself. This is the Church of God; it is the work of God alone.

Jesus spent three plus years preparing His followers for the day He would return to His Father and Their Kingdom in Heaven. He instructed the disciples in the ways of God's righteousness, the power of confession and forgiveness, how to pray and the importance of prayer. To them, Jesus gave the ability to heal the sick, cast out demons, and to preach the good news of the Saviour.

He exposed the religious ruling class as hypocrites and tools of Satan, and warned of the dangers of institutions that allow evil to be covered in religious actions, words and dogma. The evil men in these institutions were called out by Jesus for what they were: hypocrites, snakes and white-washed dwelling places of the dead. Jesus rebuked them with placing religious dogma at a greater value than God's Word and He also preached to all who would hear the hope that was now available to any who would receive it.

THE METHOD OF GOD'S LOVE

Jesus explained not the *magnitude* of God's love for His creation, but rather the *method* His love would be demonstrated to the world with the most famous words in the bible, "God so loved the world He gave His only begotten Son." A better rendering of the word "so" found in this verse is, *in this way*, not indicating a measurement, but rather a process. In the previous verses, Jesus exposes the proper understanding of verse 16 when He alluded to Moses' intervention for sin. Moses led the Jewish people out of God's Judgment by lifting up the bronze serpent. Jesus continues this comparison of the method that God prescribed to deal with the sin of the descendants of Abraham with these words, "as Moses lifted up the serpent in the wilderness, even so must the Son of man be lifted up." Jesus references this example of the lifting up of the brass serpent as the method God used to end His judgment for the sin of those who were lost in the wilderness.

This gives us a better understanding of the statement "God so loved the world," understanding not the magnitude but rather the method God would employ to demonstrate His love for His creation just "as Moses lifted up the serpent in the wilderness, even so must the Son of man be lifted up." Jesus was teaching Nicodemus and all who would seek eternal life; God sent His son to give "life and life more abundantly" by employing the method of the death and resurrection of His son. The message was clear, anyone who believed in the message of the gospel would be "born again" by God's Spirit and would have life everlasting.

Jesus came to reveal not only the love God has for His creation but Jesus also came with a message of hope for mankind. This hope for sinners was a message of repentance, forgiveness and fellowship with God. The message of the Lamb was a national call of repentance and restoration, "He came to His own and His own received Him not." When rejected by His own, Jesus preached his message of hope to all that would hear.

Jesus' message drew people by the thousands, and from the thousands many believed the message and became His disciples. From the disciples, Jesus chose and trained 12 men who would become known as "Apostles." It was to these men the message of the Gospel was entrusted and even in this assembly of the twelve there was one who opposed the message of the Saviour. It was to these men Jesus proclaimed, "...I will build My church; and the gates of hell shall not prevail against it."

THE GIFT OF THE HOLY SPIRIT

The church was taking form, but was still deep in the heart of God. Jesus prepared these men as the future leaders of His

Church. Well before the "tongues of fire" fell on these men, they were full of the Holy Spirit, as the scripture says, "he breathed on them, and saith unto them, Receive ye the Holy Ghost." Jesus, after His resurrection, would keep His promise that He would be with them always, even to the end of the world. This promise was kept by the indwelling of The Holy Spirit. "If I go not away, the Comforter will not come unto you; but if I depart, I will send him unto you."

When the work of Jesus as the Christ was completed and He was ready to return back to His Father's house, He commands the developing Church to "not depart from Jerusalem, but wait for the promise of the Father." This came to pass when the Apostles were gathered as a part of the one hundred and twenty waiting for the Saviour's promise, and the Holy Spirit indwelt them. This promise was not only fulfilled in these men but would be gifted to everyone who believed and received the Gospel message. This public demonstration of the Holy Spirit's endorsement of the church would be repeated two more times, when Apostle Peter delivered the message of the Gospel to Cornelius' and when Apostle Peter and Apostle John traveled to Samaria where Philip was preaching the Gospel.

Jesus said this indwelling would give them and us power, and this power was to be used to build His Church, "But ye shall receive power, after that the Holy Ghost is come upon you: and ye shall be witnesses unto me both in Jerusalem, and in all Judaea, and in Samaria, and unto the uttermost parts of the earth." The Holy Spirit dwells in all believers and when two or three of these Spirit-filled people gather in a single place, Jesus Himself will join in the fellowship, as it is written, "your body is the temple of the Holy Ghost which is in you, which ye have of God, and ye are not your own? For ye are bought with a price: therefore glorify God in your body, and in your spirit, which are God's." This is the Lord's Church; all the other trappings are forming the alter-ego of the church.

THE HUMAN TEMPLE

On the day of Pentecost, the one hundred and twenty gathered in faith waiting for the promise of Jesus to be delivered. These people were not fit dwelling places for God's Spirit until Jesus had completed His redemptive work, but now, they and all who would follow the Gospel message in faith would be "temples of the Holy Spirit." With the followers of Jesus now indwelt with God's Spirit, the church was delivered from the heart of God into the hearts of men.

When the Holy Spirit fell in the public, it was the endorsement of His church and the empowerment of God on all who would believe in the message of the Gospel. Not only would the followers of Jesus find peace with God in the forgiveness of sin, they would become the dwelling place of God in this world.

The Birth of the Church

John 7:37-39

...Jesus stood and cried, saying, If any man thirst, let him come unto me, and drink. He that believeth on me, as the scripture hath said, out of his belly shall flow rivers of living water. (But this spake he of the Spirit, which they that believe on him should receive: for the Holy Ghost was not yet given; because that Jesus was not yet glorified.)

Jerusalem was filled with untold thousands of men, women and children who had made the pilgrimage to celebrate the Feast of Pentecost. Forty-nine days earlier, Passover had ended with the crucifixion of Jesus and His resurrection following three days later. Jesus had instructed his disciples remain in Jerusalem and during this time Jesus, "shewed himself alive after his passion by many infallible proofs, being seen of them forty days, and speaking of the things pertaining to the kingdom of God." As Jesus taught His disciples, He instructed, "they should not depart from Jerusalem, but wait for the promise of the Father." So they waited in Jerusalem for Jesus to fulfill His promise.

It is not known how many people were in the city, but according to the Jewish historian Josephus, at a Passover during Emperor Nero's rule two million seven hundred thousand two hundred (2,700,200) persons that were pure and holy were present for the feast, and this number only included people who were ceremonially clean to join the feast. Including the Gentiles and the Jewish people who were not participating in the feast allows for countless thousands more in Jerusalem when Josephus made his count for Emperor Nero.

This feast was not the Passover but a less attended Feast of Pentecost. Still, it is probable there were hundreds of thousands if not into the millions of people in Jerusalem for this feast.

Pentecost is referenced in the Bible with different names (the Feast of Weeks, the Feast of Harvest, and the Latter First Fruits, and "Shavuot" in Hebrew, which simply means "weeks"). Pentecost was held on the fiftieth day after Passover, as a joyous time of giving thanks and presenting offerings for the new harvest grain in Israel. The name "Feast of Weeks" is derived from God's command Leviticus 23:15-16, to count seven full weeks (or 49 days) beginning on the second day of Passover, and then present offerings of new grain to the Lord as a lasting ordinance.

Pentecost is also celebrated as the Giving of the Torah to the nation of Israel, although there is no biblical imperative to support this claim, still the Jewish people teach the Torah was delivered to Moses on Mount Sinai at Pentecost. At the Passover, 50 days before Jesus was presented as the "Lamb of God," He was beaten, spat upon, tormented and ridiculed with never voicing a defense. This was not an event that would produce the intended outcome that His enemies sought after—the death of Jesus and the end of His influence in the Jewish community.

SUPERNATURAL SUPERVISION

God was and is overseeing the events in His creation. Jesus taught his disciples the value God places on sacrifices brought as offerings to Him; teaching them the value of a bird, when purchased for a sacrifice, is under the direct observation and scrutiny of God. Equipped with this knowledge, it is certain God was aware of every single action taken by each and every one who took part in the trials and execution of His Son. God was in control, the despicable intent of the enemies of Jesus was undergirded by the evil desires of Satan. Satan was seeking to once again over-throw mankind as he did in the Garden and claim victory over Jesus. Once before, Satan tried to silence Jesus' message He came to deliver. When forty days of fasting had passed in the wilderness, Satan tried and was unsuccessful to negotiate terms of surrender with Jesus. Having failed in his first attempt, Satan now tries to silence God's appointed voice in the world announcing God's plan for conquering the damage of and the wages of sin.

God Himself was in control of this episode of human history. From the detractors, liars with false testimonies, the rigged court led by the high priest Caiaphas who had prophesied, "it was expedient that one man should die for the people" and still chose to find Jesus guilty, the Roman figure-heads of Herod, Pontius Pilate who said he "found no fault in Him" yet chose to send Jesus to be crucified and the Roman soldiers who executed the sentence of death; they were all under the supervision of The Father of the Lamb. Just as Joseph affirmed, regardless of the evil objectives employed by his brothers, "God meant it for good." These evil men prepared and implemented plans to advance their power and control over humanity, but just as Joseph's brothers were but players in a plan of redemption for the nation of Israel, these men also would have their evil intents woven into the purpose that was already drafted in the hearts and minds of the Father and Son before Adam drew his first breath. If God is in direct contact with a bird bought for sacrifice, this sacrifice of His son was indeed under God's scrutiny and observation as the will of the Creator was worked out in human history.

The new harvest was without a doubt about to take place. This Pentecost, a pathway to God, would be opened not just for the Jewish people but for the people groups of the entire world. Every race, both men and women, young and old, all of humanity from the time man and woman in the Garden had failed until the last failed sinner is called home, all would be able to assemble together in full and equal fellowship with the Triune God. Soon the mystery and purpose of Jesus' arrival into this world His death and resurrection will be fully revealed and understood when the Holy Spirit gives birth to His Church. The Lord's Church would have the message of equality, anyone who would call on the name of Jesus would be saved, "Jew or Greek, male or female" would all have the same opportunity to know the Love and peace that only a right relationship with God can deliver. It would be at this Pentecost, a new covenant Jesus wrote in His own blood when He was offered as of the Lamb of God, would forever redefine the way man would gain eternal peace and fellowship with God.

REPENTANCE REQUIRED

The Old Covenant was passing away, and the New Covenant Jesus made with His disciples was soon to be released on the world, starting in Jerusalem with the outpouring of the Holy

Spirit on all who would come under the new covenant. Jesus indeed was on the threshold of fulfilling the promise, "to build My church," made to the disciples when Apostle Peter uttered, "you are the Son of the Living God." This would be a feast not a single person would ever forget. Jesus had been crucified fifty days before and many attending this feast were witnesses to the death of Jesus. They saw the unjust treatment Jesus had received. Many of the people who were celebrating the feast of Pentecost were a part of the crowd who had cried out for the release of Barabbas. They had witnessed Jesus dragging His cross to the hill where He would pay for their sin debt. They heard the words from Jesus pleading for God's forgiveness for the ones who nailed Him on the tree. It is of little surprise when the Holy Spirit fell on the followers of Jesus and Apostle Peter stood and preached Jesus' death and resurrection that many would cry out, "what shall we do?" Apostle Peter's answer was short and to the point; they had condemned Jesus to His death on the cross, they had rejected the Saviour and now had to recant their unbelief and, "Repent, and be baptized every one of you in the name of Jesus Christ for the remission of sins, and ye shall receive the gift of the Holy Ghost."

While the teaching of "baptismal regeneration" is a debate outside the scope of this book, it is important and necessary to put this statement in context with the birth of the Lord's Church. Was Peter teaching baptismal regeneration when he proclaimed "repent and be baptized?" Laying aside the arguments of grammatical structures, context and continuity of the scriptures, advocates of baptismal regeneration will focus their argument on five or six verses and of these verses only Acts 2:38 has what appears to be a commandment to be baptized as a step in reconciliation with God. If this passage is a "proof text" for the argument for baptismal regeneration, it will not stand as biblical doctrine when there is thoughtful consideration of the context in which Apostle Peter makes this statement.

Contrary to popular belief, Christianity and John the Baptist are not the originators of the baptism by immersion. When a Gentile was converted to the Jewish faith, the converts were immersed in water and were "born again," and were considered as coming from darkness into light. This was the same message John the Baptist preached in the wilderness. When the Apostle Peter proclaimed to the Jews who had rejected the Saviour, "Therefore let all the house of Israel know assuredly, that God hath made that same Jesus, whom ye have crucified, both Lord and Christ," the response of "the household of Israel" upon hearing the charge against them was that they were, "pricked in their heart, and said unto Peter and to the rest of the apostles, Men and brethren, what shall we do?" These Jews now hearing the Gospel message were convicted of "sin, righteousness and Judgment" by the Holy Spirit, and cried out *what must we do to be forgiven of the rejection of the Saviour!*

With the proper understanding of the teaching of Jewish proselytization of Gentiles and their subsequent baptism, it becomes clear Apostle Peter instructed these seekers just as John the Baptist instructed his disciples and Jesus instructed His followers about baptism. Apostle Peter told the seekers to renounce the dependence of their righteousness to secure a right relationship with God. The Jews clearly understood the intent of Apostles Peter's response to their question.

They were to publicly repent of their rejection of Jesus. Just as a Jewish proselyte was baptized as a public confession of their sinful condition and rejection of the Creator, they were to submit to baptism as a public statement revealing to the witnesses they were converted from darkness into the light and to be born again not as a Jew but as a believer and disciple of, "this same Jesus, whom ye have crucified, both Lord and Christ." The baptism Apostle Peter told the seekers to submit themselves to was not a step in salvation but a public renouncing of their rejection of the "same Jesus" who was and is, "Lord and Christ."

THE BIRTH OF THE CHURCH

When Jesus died, God ripped apart the curtain that separated the secret meeting place God had with humanity and opened up the Holy of Holies. One man, once a year, was gifted with the capacity to meet with God; now the "whosoever" who calls on the name of Jesus will not just fellowship with God, but God will make them His temple and live in them through the indwelling of the Holy Spirit. This was the birth of the church, when the Holy Spirit arrived as "cloves of fire." It was pure, unadulterated and free of any constructs made by men. This is the Church of God. Anything we add creating the institution must enhance, not distract, from what God has established as His Church.

Indeed, the Holy Spirit gave them power to preach. Thousands upon thousands were exposed to the message of salvation, and thousands received God's Gift of everlasting life. The Church now born has only one identity. There were not groups gathering in permanent locations, no "doctrinal distinctives." The message of salvation along with the infilling of the Holy Spirit was all that brought these people together as the church. Hungry to know more about Jesus and His Church, people gathered every day, house to house, in the temple, and any other place where they could assemble to learn more of the Saviour. The church was multiplying every day, with people who confessed Christ and had received the gift of the Holy Spirit. God's Spirit empowered them to be witnesses to the people who desired to hear about the risen Saviour. The Pentecost attenders now sought to know more of their Saviour they had rejected.

The Church preached a message of Jesus, His crucifixion and resurrection, with an invitation for all to repent of their unbelief. Their unbelief had caused them to reject Jesus and call for His crucifixion, fifty days before when Jesus payed the price for their sin at Golgotha. They were numbered among the scoffers; now they could stand with the redeemed.

The new-born church grew rapidly, and the new followers of the Risen Saviour were hungry for the teachings of the Apostles. Many of the new believers and seekers of the Lord Jesus did not return to their own homes after Pentecost's final days. They gathered in fellow believers' homes, in the temple courts and wherever else they could gather to hear God's words concerning what had happened to them and how to serve their new found friend they had in Jesus. There was no argument over what day of the week they would worship God. There was no "Sunday" worshipers and there was no "Sabbath day" worshipers there was only the "everyday worshipers." Great need grew with the rapid growth of the church. People who had not returned home were running low on food, widows who stayed with the people of God were now disenfranchised from their families that had returned home. A great need was filled by a great work of God.

THE COMMUNAL CHURCH

The only place this communal behavior is found in the New Testament Church is in the events following the birth of the Lord's church. The Holy Spirit was alive and well in the Church in Jerusalem. Homes were opened to brothers and sisters in Christ; many brought their possessions and they were sold with the proceeds given to the apostles to distribute as needs arose.

These gifts were not for "operational expenses," rather, these gifts were intended for the direct needs of the new believers who had stayed in Jerusalem after they were born-again. The church had no need for church treasurers, finance committees, budgets or outside accountant reviews. There were no building payments, utility bills, no youth funds and no paid staff. There were no Christian collages, no seminaries, no mission boards and no retirement funds. The pastoral staff (the apostles) did not send in résumés to a pastor search committee, nor was there was not a Doctor of Ministry degree among them. The pastors of this church were not equipped to do this work by men but rather by the work of the Holy Spirit, and the work of the church was blessed by God, embraced by the redeemed, and hated by the world.

God's church was not and is not filled with perfect people. As afore alluded, even in the twelve Jesus chose it is recorded that Judas was a devil. In this new church there were some who were committed born-again followers of Jesus—Philip and Stephen shine as bright examples of those who lived committed lives. Philip who became a great evangelist for the Lord's church and Stephen whose life and ministry was cut short under a pile of stones.

The institution that was growing around the church also brought in imitators of the true followers of Jesus. Ananias and Sapphira will always be held in contempt for their deception. They will always be known for their attempt to receive the rewards and blessings given to the true members of the Lord's Church with having only an identification to the church's alter-ego.

This newly formed institution of the church began to experience dissatisfaction among its members, not with the message of the Gospel or with the doctrines as taught by the Apostles, but conflict within the institution of the church. Numerical growth brought about the need for structural development to accommodate the demands of the people. Ministries were developing around the needs and were empowered to fill the growing needs in the church. A new ministry was developed around the distribution of the gifts that were delivered to the Apostles for the rising needs of the growing church. Even the best solutions deployed in the institution of the church are stained with the efforts of saved sinners, the methods and practices of daily ministrations of food were causing conflict in the fellowship of the believers.

The Lord's Church was preaching the Gospel in homes, at the temple and in the public square. Some were saved and some rejected the message. The ones who were delivering the message of hope experienced persecution, sometimes even to death, as Stephen who gave his life preaching hope to the hopelessly lost.

THE FIRST INSTITUTION

As the institution was being built around the church, we see growing personal conflicts, imperfect ministries/ministers, and even the evil works of the likes of Ananias and his wife Sapphira.

The collection of Christians had been organized into a church. The church at Jerusalem is the first instance that can be documented where the forming of the institution of the church was over-shadowing the Lord's Church. Ministries were developed; the giving of gifts of property, goods and monies gave need for appointed servants. These servants were selected to provide a resolution for the dissention between believers, as well as oversite of the distribution of the new found "assets" of the church.

These servants were not involved in the propagation of the message of the church. These appointments were made to provide fair and equal treatment to all who associated with the believers. The Apostles, in petitioning the members of the Church in Jerusalem for their approval of this decision, reveal how the institution of the Church was shaped—not just by the Apostles, but by the members of the church as well.

The seven who were selected were overseen by the church leadership and we see reflections of the congregation taking part in determining how the institution was to grow around the Lord's Church. Peter's statement, in giving the resolution for the distractions that the assets and their distribution triggered, sums up the purpose of this institution coming into existence when he says, "It is not reason that we should leave the word of God, and serve tables."

The Gospel message and the commission given to the Church by Jesus is the purpose for Lord's Church. The institution that is co-joined should not be a distraction to the God-given purpose for the existence of the Lord's Church, but should assist the church pastors and members prepare and dispatch the Gospel to the "World" for whom Jesus had shed His blood.

The Church in Jerusalem soon faced great persecution and

would end the need, for the larger part, the institution of the church. Soon only the Twelve would be left and the institution that was built around the needs of the congregation would dissolve. Certainly the Twelve did not call a business meeting to appoint one of themselves to replace the seven men selected to "wait tables," nor did they come up with a new church vision to bring in new people to support and rebuild the institution that was now totally collapsed. The Lord's Church was still in Jerusalem but the institution was no longer there.

Across America, institutions of the Church are open for business, but the Lord's Church is not there. Many church institutions have taken on a life of their own, the need that required the institution has passed but still the institution exists. The institutions are still alive; people, buildings, staff and programs, but the Lord's Church has moved on, leaving behind the institution built around the Lord's Church. The work of the Holy Spirit is no longer required for their survival. They have programs, paid staff, music leaders, outreach programs, people-centric ministries, children and youth programs, and money in the bank. They still have the name of the Church, but they are just sleepwalking in a dream of the past. The Lord adds to His church and people build the institutions. The Lord's Church is built from the redemption of lost sinners and the church's institutions are built with warm bodies and financial gifts from the community.

When the *Lord's Church* changes directions, it simply considers the leadership of the Holy Spirit. When the *institution of the church* changes directions, it must consider assets, ministries, personnel and financial changes. If the church institution is focused on families, youth, and social ministries, the assets will be consumed supporting and building these programs as a means of bringing more people into the institution with the assumption the Lord's Church is benefiting as well. There is a real danger of the institution shifting the focus from the Gospel of Jesus Christ to supporting the numerical and financial growth of the institution. The doctrinal teachings and exclusivity of the Gospel of Jesus will be sequestered for the purpose of bringing more people into the church institution. Removing the core teachings of the bible on issues of morality and sin, and salvation can advance the growth of the churches institutions, but will grieve the Lord's Church.

PERSECUTION: THE TWO-EDGED SWORD

Saul of Tarsus had arrived in Jerusalem. Upon his arrival, Saul oversaw the stoning of Stephen. He had been commissioned to gather up and carry away the believers, and now he was making havoc in the Jerusalem Church. After Stephen was executed, Saul went from house to house collecting the followers of Jesus and sending a chilling fear in the hearts of the new converts prompting them to flee the city for protection. They fled from Saul, but not from Jesus and their newfound faith. The Lord's Church left behind the established institution of the Church and scattered in different groups and places.

All left except the Apostles, they remained behind protected by God for a season. This great mass of Christians scattered in the regions of Judea, Samaria, Phenice, Cyprus, and Antioch. Indeed, Satan in his attempt to destroy the work of the Saviour, was doing the bidding of the Heavenly Father. This new found Church consisted for the most part of Jewish converts and there was a strong identity with the city of Jerusalem, temple worship, and the traditions of the Fathers.

God's plan for the Gospel was not to be confined to Jerusalem but be spread to Judea and then to the "uttermost parts of the earth." Satan's attempt to overthrow God's people only served to enlarge the Christian movement. Joseph's words once again ring true, "you meant it for evil but God meant it for good." Good thus came out of evil; and Saul's persecution gave rise to, as all following attempts to destroy the Lord's Church have, progressing the cause which it was intended to destroy. To the opponents of the Christian movement, the persecution led by Saul of Tarsus appeared to have considerably damaged the Lord's Church. In reality, only the institution of the church suffered any damage; the Lord's Church grew numerically and spiritually during this time. It is of the utmost importance for a follower of Jesus to understand, identify, and separate institutional success and failure from the Lord's Church.

It was during this time Jesus met with Saul on the Damascus road and not only ended the terror he struck in the hearts of Christians, but also would be the beginning of a new alter-ego the new church would soon have.

For a time, the church of Jerusalem's institution would lay in waste. When the Church would rebuild in Jerusalem, a new institution would be built based on the current needs that would arise, not on past needs or ideas of ministry. The ability to follow the Lord and His Church often requires the ability to walk away from the institutions men build around the true Church.

UNEQUALLY YOKED

To have the ability to separate the church and the institutions built around her, allows believers to invest in the Lord's Church and when called for, to oppose or abandon the institution of the church without experiencing shame or heartache. When the institution is no longer supporting the mission and purpose it was created to assist, the believers must rebuild the institution or abandon it.

Promoting the institutions of the church as building the Kingdom of God has been used for centuries to establish the importance of buildings and large membership rolls. The understanding offered by many Christian groups that building the Kingdom of God is equivalent to growing the church's institution is false; building a building, having large crowds or amassing assets does not advance the Kingdom of God. Jesus said His Kingdom was not on earth. Advancing the Kingdom of God only happens when the Gospel of Jesus is preached and names are added to the Lamb's Book of Life. When the church's institution has a purpose which differs from that of the Lord's Church, there often is an attempt to co-mingle the mission and purpose of the institution with the mission of the church. This co-mingling has often infiltrated the church's institutions to justify the use of the majority of the time, wealth and attention of the members to build the institutions instead of the Lord's church. To validate this statement, all that is necessary is to look where the monies are going in a church budget. If fifty percent or more of the total offerings are going to non-great commission activities like staff salaries, building payments, building upkeep and program funding, this institution has usurped the purpose of the Lord's Church.

The Shaping of the Church at the Hands of the Apostles

Matthew 16:15-18

...whom say ye that I am? And Simon Peter answered and said,
Thou art the Christ, the Son of the living God...
upon this rock I will build my church;
and the gates of hell shall not prevail against it.

Saul had a life-changing experience with Jesus and soon would find a new purpose for his life. Saul's encounter with Jesus came by revelation and his new-found relationship with God was established in faith. Living in faith when God reveals Himself will establish a believer in a way of life corresponding with God's purpose, allowing a Christian to find and follow after His will. When following after God's purpose, God will put the right person, at the right time, with the right words to guide His people where He wants them to be, and properly equip them to do the work He has planned.

Finding God's way in life is not necessarily achieved by knowing the end of God's purpose before following after it. Faith is the currency used to please God, for as the scripture says, "without faith it is impossible to please Him." For a believer, discovering God's purpose is a journey of faith, faith that gives structure to hold God's people on course until His purpose is fully revealed. Faith is the proof that a Christian looks to when there is no substance to place trust in, as it has been conveyed in the scripture, "faith is the substance of things hoped for and the evidence of things not seen." When living a life of faith, God arranges events that will guide His followers to places and people that He will use to propel them forward as they seek to know His planned purpose. It only takes a backwards glance in the life of a faithful believer to expose God's fingerprints of involvement as He guides a life lived in faith. God will place people, resources, and understanding before the "faith walkers" to reveal understanding and to provide wisdom and direction in the life a believer.

Stricken blind, Saul is motivated by faith as he was led on a journey to Damascus to the house of Judas. There he prayed seeking God's purpose for his life after meeting with Jesus. Not only would Saul receive understanding, but his next encounter on his new journey with Jesus would restore his sight.

AN ENEMY BECOMES A BROTHER

At the same time Saul was fasting and praying for answers, the Holy Spirit was moving in the heart of Ananias, a disciple of Jesus, to seek out Saul. Just as God prepared Ananias to find and bring Saul into his home, God had revealed to Ananias that God was preparing a great ministry for Saul of Tarsus, he was told by God's Spirit, "he is a chosen vessel unto me, to bear my name before the Gentiles, and kings, and the children of Israel." Ananias travels to Judas' house and greets Saul with Christian identification, "brother," and engages in Christian fellowship with Saul. Ananias, as moved by the Holy Spirit accepted this one-time enemy of the Church of God as now a brother in Christ.

Paul will later understand and expound on his experience with Jesus that gives a better understanding of his acceptance by Ananias. To the Corinthian Church, Paul explains what Jesus' revelation did for him and Ananias in their encounter, "Therefore if any man be in Christ, he is a new creature: old things are passed away; behold, all things are become new. And all things are of God, who hath reconciled us to himself by Jesus Christ, and hath given to us the ministry of reconciliation." Saul had become a new creation and Ananias took on the ministry of reconciliation as he embraced Saul in his new found Christian birth.

After Ananias and Paul establish a relationship as brothers in Christ, Paul will spend three years in Arabia where Jesus personally instructs him not only in doctrine but also of God's purpose in delivering him from his sin and the eventual conclusion of his ministry. Paul was soon to find his path in the service of Jesus who had saved him, but first he will experience character building, adversity, and the not so gentle hand of guidance to lead him back home where he started his misguided crusade against the Lord's Church.

Saul, now known as Paul, returns on his journey to Damascus but this time he was not "breathing out threatenings and slaughter against the disciples of the Lord" as the avenger of God against the followers of Jesus. This journey would establish Christian unity between Paul and the disciples in their worship and service of the Lord. The enthusiasm applied by Saul when he was trying to destroy the Christian community now was transferred into a new life purpose of Christian love and ministry.

Paul had a burden for his Jewish brothers, his desire was to help the Jewish people to understand and experience the transformation that changed not only his mind about Jesus, but his relationship with God. Paul was driven by his new-found understanding of God's love to preach Jesus with unrestrained vigor. Paul's love for his people was so great he said, "That I have great heaviness and continual sorrow in my heart. For I could wish that myself were accursed from Christ for my brethren, my kinsmen according to the flesh." Paul was filled with the Holy Spirit and he desired to bring his new-found hope of redemption to others. His preaching was so intense and powerful, he was soon experiencing the same anger and fear that he had delivered to others.

Escaping in a basket lowered over the city's wall, Paul makes his way to Jerusalem and, after Barnabas vouches for the authenticity of his conversion, was introduced to James the brother of Jesus. There he preached with the disciples for two weeks where his disputes with the Grecians were so powerful that the Grecians sought to kill him. Paul escaped death and went home to Tarsus. In this same interval of time, God was preparing the way for Paul's future mission work to the Gentiles.

PETER'S CONFESSION

The tenth chapter of the book of Acts is the pivot point of the church. God opens the way of faith and salvation to the Gentiles, who would be assimilated into the Lord's Church. God had opened the same door of faith and salvation to the Jewish people through the preaching of Apostle Peter, and the Samaritans found the way to the Saviour when Philip preached to them the Gospel he had learned from the teachings of the Apostle Peter.

When the church in Jerusalem became aware of the Samaritan's acceptance of the Gospel message, Apostles Peter and John were sent to validate the work in Samaria that Philip had started. Apostle Peter preaches the entire message of the Gospel, and then the Holy Spirit indwelt the Samaritans just as it had happened in Jerusalem. This, in conjunction with Apostle Peter's rooftop experience, was evidence the Gospel was about to be opened to the Gentiles.

While Apostle Peter was praying in Joppa on Simon's rooftop, God revealed to him in a vision that Peter was chosen to establish God's approval of the "whosoever" becoming a part of His Church. In this vision Peter "saw heaven opened, and a certain vessel descending upon him, as it had been a great sheet knit at the four corners, and let down to the earth wherein were all manner of four-footed beasts of the earth, and wild beasts, and creeping things, and fowls of the air." When God said to him, "Rise, Peter; kill, and eat," Peter responded he would never violate the Jewish command against eating unclean animals. With Peter's rejection came a warning from God, "What God hath cleansed, that call not thou common." Just to make sure Peter understood the intent of this encounter with God, He repeated the vision three times. God would soon validate this vision given to Peter, affirming the Gentiles were to be included in His Church.

At the same time Apostle Peter was praying, so was Cornelius. Cornelius was a Gentile who served as a Centurion in the Italian Regiment. He and all his family feared God and provided assistance to people in need and prayed to God regularly. In his prayer time, Cornelius had a vision of an Angel of God who affirmed his desire to know God had been acknowledged. The Angel of

God said, "Thy prayers and thine alms are come up for a memorial before God." In this vision Cornelius was instructed to send for Apostle Peter.

THE "UNIVERSAL" OR CATHOLIC CHURCH

The opportunity of salvation through the cross of Jesus was soon to be opened to the "utter most part of the world." With this, the Holy Spirit gave these words to Apostle Peter, "Of a truth I perceive that God is no respecter of persons: But in every nation he that feared him, and worketh righteousness, is accepted with him." God opens the avenue of the cross to the world for whom His son had died.

As the Apostle Peter preaches the Gospel of Jesus to Cornelius and the many who were assembled with him, salvation came to all who would believe and the Holy Spirit gave visual evidence just as He did in Jerusalem and Samaria.

God's endorsement when gifting the Gentiles with the Holy Spirit, gave evidence of God's approval that the Gospel was to be preached to all people groups and indeed they were accepted by God. The believing Jews who accompanied the Apostle Peter gave consent for water baptism to validate the acceptance of the Gentiles into the Lord's Church. Peter was not the first Pope of the Lord's Church as embraced and taught by the Catholics. Peter was given only the mission of providing Jewish approval of the Gentile's acceptance in the Lord's Church.

Peter's ministry would be both to and for the Jewish people, with only a little future interaction with the non-Jewish people groups. We can be certain of this, no biblical or secular evidence exists that reveals that the Apostle Peter ever made a trip to

Rome, much less to have pastored the Roman Church. Catholic teachings that place both Apostle Peter and Paul together founding the Church in Rome and as well Catholic teachings claiming both were crucified together in Rome are not supported in the New Testament, church or secular history. These claims are made without any secular or biblical evidence, and are, in fact, in contradiction to the Apostle Paul's writing to Timothy when he stated only Luke was with him as he awaited his execution.

God had called and prepared the Apostle Paul to be the one who would bring the message of hope, love, and redemption to the Gentiles. God in His wisdom gave a natural division in the soon to be formed institutions of the Jewish and Gentile Churches that would dispel any teaching of a "Universal" or Catholic Church collective to be practiced on this side of heaven.

The church groups existed independent from each other, except when providing mission or benevolence assistance. There is no evidence in the New Testament Churches of a single point of authority. The fact has been established that God had appointed at least two different divisions with the Apostle Paul and Peter with separate ministry objectives. God had established Paul as the Apostle to the Gentiles, and Peter as the Apostle to the Jews; this division in church identity is affirmed with these words spoken by Paul, "For he that wrought effectually in Apostle Peter to the apostleship of the circumcision, the same was mighty in me toward the Gentiles."

When observing the church in the times of the Apostles, it is easy to see there existed two distinct and separate identities that were being formed. The churches identifying with the Apostle Paul's work were comprised of mostly Gentile converts and the churches identifying with the Apostle Peter's work were comprised mostly of Jewish converts. In these diverse cultures, the Lord's Church is established and built.

The same Gospel, Holy Spirit and Saviour had added all of the redeemed into the Lord's Church, as the scripture says, "For ye are all the children of God by faith in Christ Jesus. For as many of you as have been baptized into Christ have put on Christ. There is neither Jew nor Greek, there is neither bond nor free, there is neither male nor female: for ye are all one in Christ Jesus. And if ye be Christ's, then are ye Abraham's seed, and heirs according to the promise." If in Lord's Church there is not Jew or Greek why is there a difference established in the identities in the biblical account of the development of the Church? The differences enumerated are not reflected in fellowship with the Lord Jesus but rather in the establish divisions in the institutions of the church in the New Testament.

The reality of God's approval for numerous identities in the institutions should dispel any acceptance of a catholic structure in the church's institutions. It is a biblical imperative that in the Lord's Church, all are equal and received into God's grace by the same sacrifice made by the founder and Lord of the Church, Jesus. There will be a single church entity when the entire collective of the Church of the Lord stands before Him in heaven. Until then there has, and will continue to be different institutions hosting His church on earth.

DUAL IDENTITY

It is unmistakably evident there were separate identities developing between the Jewish and non-Jewish church groups. The Lord's Church, when joined with the different institutional identities, creates an alter-ego. There is an inherent danger of having an institutional identity—often there is a co-mingling of the requirements of membership in the institution with the salvation message of the Gospel. It is the nature of all institutions to grow and create structure to provide management and to regulate behavior in the group. Often when these structural establishments are implemented, they will differ from biblical teachings.

The unintended consequence of institutional growth is the danger of the creation of a separate identity that will over-shadow the Lord's Church. The alter-ego will develop its own ideology, rules, and laws that not only establishes an identity, but will also regulate membership requirements into that group and establish guidelines for acceptable behavior.

Leaders of the institution will seek to enforce standards, laws, and ideologies as requirements to be in good standing with the institution, and often confuses acceptance in the institution as equal to acceptance in the Lord's Church. As this structure formed both in the Jewish and non-Jewish church identities, ideologies and practices differed. Although there is an acceptance of the structure of the institution, even if the structure is commonly accepted by the group as a whole, it does not allow for the message of the Gospel to be adulterated. As the different institutions of the Church were forming, they would develop differences in their doctrine, ideology, and practices as the churches were birthed. The discrepancies between the different institutions would cause strife and bring about questions concerning the different practices and doctrines that were developing as the separate identities were established as church groups.

The different institutions were evangelizing the lost. Apostle Peter and the churches established from his work were reaching the lost mostly in Jerusalem, Samaria and Judea. Apostle Paul was sent by God on his missionary work that would lead him throughout the lands held by the Gentiles. Paul went on three missionary journeys; in these trips many coastal cities and trade route towns were the focus of his preaching and many church groups were established under his leadership.

The Apostle Paul and Barnabas began their missionary journey preaching in the town Synagogues. With many of the Jews rejecting Paul's preaching of Christ, and seeking to do harm to Apostle Paul and Barnabas, God revealed to the Apostle Paul he was to go and preach the Gospel to the lands of the Gentiles exclusively. As the scripture tells us, "the Lord commanded us, saying, I have set thee to be a light of the Gentiles, that thou shouldest be for salvation unto the ends of the earth." Paul would bring the Gospel to Greece, Philippi, Athens, Antioch, Syria Seleucia, Syria, Cyprus, Asia Minor, Cilicia, Lycaonia, Phrygia, Galatia, Mysia and Rome and other places as well.

As they were established, each of the churches began to build out their own institutional identity. Each church group would create an institution, with each having a different identity that would be shaped by the environment and culture where people lived. Those who were saved and added to the church were to help mold the institution.

The institutions of the Church reflect: the people, culture, economy, demographics and political environment of the people groups and places the institutions are established. As doctrinal and institutional distinctives are developed, walls of ideology are built. These ideological walls help secure the loyalty of its members and will not only give each church institution a different identity but often places the church institutions in conflict with other institutions of the church. These institutional walls serve two purposes. The more powerful of the two are the walls of separation that church institutions build to create an environment of dependency for the institution in matters of salvation and service. These walls create an environment of fear, to keep the members of the institution in subjection to the leadership and the requirements of the institution, to be in good standing at the risk of eternal damnation. The second wall of separation is designed to "evangelize" the other church institutions, often with verbal and physical abuse, into accepting the institutional distinctives, there-by growing its influence and power.

RECOGNIZING THE DIFFERENCE

The Lord's Church reflects the teachings of the Apostles. Biblical based polity, doctrines and practices based on the scripture, not man's dogma, and the great commission will drive all her activities. A continuity exists between the different local assemblies of the Lord's Church that will advance fellowship, unity, and cooperation for the common cause of Christ. In contrast, it is often the nature of the institutions of the church to build walls of separation between the different institutions. For the most part, these walls of separation are built with non-scriptural practices and requirements that will make the relationship with institution important, often more important than the Lord's Church in matters of worship, service, and salvation.

The building of the church found in the New Testament came at a high cost to the believers. Not one of the many martyrs who laid down their life did so for the institutions, they gave all they had to offer for the Lord's Church and the Gospel of the Apostles. The institutions of the church come and go; they rise in power and prominence and fade in from the history of humanity. The promise Jesus made concerning the gates of hell's ability to overcome was not made to the institutions of the church. History records many of the church institutions rising and falling in the church history, but the promise Jesus made was made to His Church, and she is standing secure and steady long after the rise and fall of her institutions. Church tradition records that the followers of the Lord's Church that founded and established her suffered greatly, the following list reveals the price paid by many of them:

- **Matthew** in Ethiopia was killed by a sword wound.
- **Mark** was dragged by horses through the streets until he was dead.
- **Luke** (Paul's doctor who joined Paul on his missionary journeys) was hanged in Greece as a result of his tremendous preaching to the lost.
- **John** was boiled in oil and survived, only to be sentenced to the mines on the prison Island of Patmos.
- **Peter** was crucified upside down.
- **James** was thrown over a hundred feet down from the southeast pinnacle of the Temple. He survived the fall, but was then beaten to death with a club.
- **James the Son of Zebedee** was beaten to death with a whip.
- **Andrew** was crucified.
- **Thomas** was stabbed with a spear.
- **Jude** was killed with arrows.
- **Matthias** was stoned and then beheaded.
- **Paul** was tortured and then beheaded.

- **Simon the Zealot** was sawn in half.
- **Philip** was tortured and then crucified upside down.

In the book of Hebrews, Apostle Paul uses the servants of God in the Old Testament to demonstrate that His people do suffer at the hands of the enemy even though they had "obtained a good report through faith," but still "received not the promise (the promise made to Abraham)." Apostle Paul narrated their experiences with, "They were stoned, they were sawn asunder, were tempted, were slain with the sword: they wandered about in sheepskins and goatskins; being destitute, afflicted, tormented; Of whom the world was not worthy: they wandered in deserts, and in mountains, and in dens and caves of the earth."

The difference between the sufferings of the people of faith before the coming of the Saviour, and the people of faith under the new testament written in the blood of Jesus is: *the blood of Jesus paid the price for sin and paved a way for the "whosoever" to be added to the Lamb's Book of Life.* To escape the sword or die by the sword did not determine the victory, but rather faith placed in the "Gift" of God was the victory. The Holy Spirit's indwelling added to the Church all who would believe and confess in the blood atonement of Jesus, and the blood was spilt and will continue to be spilt in martyrdom of untold thousands of followers of Jesus. This would be the foundation of the Lord's Church as it is known today in the world.

Any Other Gospel

CHAPTER
4

Galatians 1:8

But though we, or an angel from heaven, preach any other gospel unto you than that which we have preached unto you, let him be accursed.

The first challenge for the Lord's Church was, is, and always will be keeping the Gospel of Jesus without adulteration. Satan and his cohorts are always chipping away at the Gospel. The first institutional attempt to suppress the message of the Lord's Church was by Jewish Synagogue leadership. In an attempt to contain the growth of the Lord's Church, the Synagogue's leadership launched an effort on the behalf of the Jewish leaders to co-opt the church into the Synagogue worship.

Paul often went and was welcomed into the Synagogues to preach Jesus, "...as his manner was, went in unto them, and three Sabbath days reasoned with them out of the scriptures, Opening and alleging, that Christ must needs have suffered, and risen again from the dead; and that this Jesus, whom I preach unto you, is Christ. And some of them believed, and consorted with Paul and Silas; and of the devout Greeks a great multitude, and of the chief women not a few."

When this attempt to co-opt the Lord's Church was not successful, the Council of Jamnia was called in 95 AD and gathered to determine the relationship the Synagogue would have with the Lord's Church. The outcome of this council was, what is known as the Twelfth Benediction. The.Twelfth Benediction was a document that was drafted and was approved and reads in part: "And may the Nazarenes [Christians] and heretics perish quickly." Consequently, the Council drew a bright line between Christianity and Judaism. Any Jew who became a Christian was unwelcome in the Synagogues and often be persecuted for their faith.

In the year 30 AD, Christianity mainly consisted of Jews who accepted Jesus as the Messiah. By the year 100 AD, Christianity consisted mainly of Gentiles. This, in part, can be attributed to the travels of the Apostle Paul which increasingly focused on Gentiles, along with the Jews' persecution increasingly forcing the Jewish Christians out of the Synagogues leaving them in disarray.

Conflicts began to surface in church teachings between the different institutions of the church in the first century. The doctrines of the Lord's Churches came from the Apostle Paul's teachings to the Gentile-established churches and the teachings of the Apostle Peter to the Jewish-established Churches. The same Gospel for all the Lord's Churches, and the same doctrines for all the Lord's Churches; there was no difference in the teachings of salvation, sanctification and justification in the churches established in Jewish or Gentile locations. As the institutions of the church began to take shape, it can be seen they were developing a difference in practices and ideology in the Jewish and Gentile church institutions. These differences would cause conflicts and sometimes divisions in in the churches Apostles Paul and Peter planted and nurtured in the first century.

CHURCH MEMBERSHIP

The evidence of the unsaved having an identity in the churches institutions is evident in many of the writings of the Apostles. One such account is found when the Apostle Paul travels to Jerusalem with Barnabas a Jew who was converted to Christianity from Judaism, and Titus a Gentile who was a convert to Christianity from heathenism. Paul said he made this trip by "revelation" to meet with the leaders of the Jerusalem Church and presented Titus and Barnabas as evidence of the work of the Holy Spirit in his ministry.

Apostle Paul reveals to the brethren in Jerusalem there were unsaved men who were members of the institution of the church in Jerusalem. He exposes the lost members when he recounts the experience he had while he was there, "But neither Titus, who was with me, being a Greek, was compelled to be circumcised: And that because of false brethren unawares brought in, who came in privily to spy out our liberty which we have in Christ Jesus, that they might bring us into bondage." The lost members of the institution of the church in Jerusalem violated common decency and became perverted voyeurs in observing the disrobing of Titus. The institution of the church breached biblical teachings and common courtesy in the name of Christianity. As well, institutions housing the church groups established by Apostle

Paul in the Gentile lands had their share of unbelieving members, as the scripture says, "They went out from us, but they were not of us; for if they had been of us, they would no doubt have continued with us: but they went out, that they might be made manifest that they were not all of us."

It is an established fact that unsaved members of the New Testament churches institutions established membership requirements, having no effect on becoming a part of the Lord's Church, and demanded enforcement even if they caused division in the Lord's Church.

It is also a fact that a false believer can be in good standing with the institution built around the Lord's Church, but only the blood bought born-again Spirit indwelt believer is welcomed in the Church of the living God.

This meeting Apostle Paul had with the Church in Jerusalem established the singularity of the Lord's Church, and existence of the plurality of church identities. The outcome of this meeting affirmed the fellowship of the believers and recognized differences in institutions the churches were establishing were both legitimate and hosted the Lord's Church. The difference in the institutions of these two offshoots of the Lord's Church was clearly seen. The Jewish traditions had influenced the identity of the believers in the Jerusalem Church and this identity was not a requirement for salvation and acceptance in the Lord's Church. It is recorded by Apostle Paul that after this meeting, it was established, "the Gospel of the uncircumcision was committed unto me, as the Gospel of the circumcision was unto Apostle Peter;" peace was made and given was "the right hands of fellowship; that we should go unto the heathen, and they unto the circumcision."

There were different cultures that the true church was built from and from these cultures arose an institutional environment the churches existed in. Apostles Paul and Peter both acknowledged the existence of the institution of the church, but declared the institutions ideology or practices did not have the authority to overrule the Lord's Church in her doctrines and practices.

REMNANTS OF TRADITION

Not long after this meeting the Apostle Peter returns Apostle Paul's visit with a journey to Antioch to observe the Gentile church. While the Apostle Peter was staying with the believers, he joined with them to eat a meal. This was strictly forbidden in the institution of church led by him. Apostle Peter's own words declared this Jewish tradition was superseded by God when he meant with Cornelius. When Apostle Peter arrived at Cornelius house Apostle Peter said, "Ye know how that it is an unlawful thing for a man that is a Jew to keep company, or come unto one of another nation; but God hath shewed me that I should not call any man common or unclean."

In the freedom of the Spirit of God, and in the name of Christian fellowship, Apostle Peter joins with the born again Jews and Gentiles for a fellowship meal. Apostle Peter was unaware that James and other men from the church of Jerusalem decided to make this same journey to visit the Church in Antioch. When James and the others walked in on the fellowship meal Apostle Peter was shocked and surprised. His response was so intense that when he withdrew. The other Jews, including Barnabas who was a missionary with Paul to this community, withdrew as well. Barnabas, who had preached, loved, and perhaps baptized some of these people separated from them along with the other Jews because of Apostle Peter's response to the arrival of James.

Paul was angered and broken at the same time. When Paul was informed of Apostle Peter's hypocrisy, he spoke these words to Apostle Peter in the presence of all who were at this meal, "If thou, being a Jew, livest after the manner of Gentiles, and not as do the Jews, why compellest thou the Gentiles to live as do the Jews?...Knowing that a man is not justified by the works of the law, but by the faith of Jesus Christ, even we have believed in Jesus Christ, ...for by the works of the law shall no flesh be justified ...I am crucified with Christ: nevertheless I live; yet not I, but Christ liveth in me: and the life which I now live in the flesh I live by the faith of the Son of God, who loved me, and gave himself for me. I do not frustrate the grace of God: for if righteousness come by the law, then Christ is dead in vain."

It is apparent from this account, that even though a settlement of the ideology between the Jewish churches and the Gentile churches was agreed upon in the meeting with Apostles Paul and Peter in Jerusalem, it did not change the institution of the Jerusalem Church. It is clear Apostle Peter continued to practice, after Paul left Jerusalem, the accepted standards set by the institution concerning the Gentiles and Jewish separation. When the Apostle Paul confronted Apostle Peter with his allegiance to the institution in Jerusalem and not the Lord's Church, Peter, "withdrew" or surrendered to Paul in his failure in keeping the Lord's Church's teachings over the institutional teachings of Jerusalem.

The difference in worship, practice and application of the Jewish law had created separate identities in these different faith communities that was powerful enough that Apostle Peter himself felt obligated to conform to the institutional ideology of not eating with Gentiles even though Jesus had revealed to him there were no restrictions based on nationality or race concerning the fellowship of faith in Jesus. The power of the institution to change the nature and purpose of the Lord's Church is exposed by the fact that the Apostle Peter himself found institutional acceptance a powerful force that overshadowed even his personal encounter with Jesus over the acceptance of the Gentiles in the Lord's Church.

A casual reading of Apostle Paul's letters to the churches that found their way into the canonized scripture uncovers alter-egos of the different churches. The institutions growing around these fellowships are often the focus of Apostle Paul's corrective criticism. The church in Corinth's acceptance of immoral behavior was established in the institution that developed around the Lord's Church. In the Church at Galicia, legalism and Gnosticism were developed around the alter-ego of the Lord's Church. In the Church of Laodicea, prosperity was developed around the Lord's Church, and the list goes on. Establishing the church as an "institution" is not difficult to perceive, and it is not unreasonable to conclude the "alter-ego" of the institution these churches took. Not only the energy and identity was robbed from the Lord's Church, but this alter-ego was the cause of many in these fellowships to accept false doctrine and often defend not only the evil practices of unsaved members of the institution, but even endorse their behavior.

The different alter-egos the first century churches were forming often degraded the teachings of the Apostles. When this happened, the practices and the ones practicing these teachings were confronted and exposed by the Apostles. The Church in Corinth built in the heart of heathenism, was less than fifty miles from

Athens where idolatry was so prevalent it was said, "it is easier to find a god than a man in Athens." Corinth was significantly influenced by the culture of Athens, and the Church of God was built from converts of this idolatrous community. The culture of the church in Corinth developed with these idolatrous behaviors finding their way into the practices of the church. The institution that the church existed in was so detrimental to the true church, it almost destroyed their identity with the righteousness of Christ.

When the Apostle Paul became aware of their practices, he warned them that God's chastisement was causing sickness and even death among the members of the Church. The institutions of the churches of Galicia came under the influence of teachers of the Mosaic Law insisting the work of Christ was incomplete without the adherence to the embodiment of law found in the Torah. The Apostle Paul rebuked the culture of the Churches with this warning, "Though we, or an angel from heaven, preach any other Gospel unto you than that which we have preached unto you, let him be accursed. As we said before, so say I now again, if any man preach any other Gospel unto you than that ye have received, let him be accursed."

It is the teachings of the Apostles, whom Jesus said would be reminded by the Holy Spirit of all the words He had spoken, as well the special revelations from God given to them, that must establish the true identity of the Lord's Church. It is recorded in the scripture, "And the Lord added to the Church daily such as should be saved." The true Church has a "membership roll," it is identified as the "Lamb's Book of Life." The institution that develops around the true Church also has a membership roll, first found in the Catholic Church institution, and the "members" may or may not be in the Lamb's Book of Life.

The identity of the true Church of God is found not in its ideology, but in the keeping of the teachings of the Apostles. It is possible the alter-ego of the church can overtake the identity of the true Church. Jesus warns of the consequences when this failure occurs in His warning to the churches in Ephesus if they did not reform and return to the established teachings of the Apostles. Jesus says, "Remember therefore from whence thou art fallen, and repent, and do the first works; or else I will come unto thee quickly, and will remove thy candlestick out of his place, except thou repent."

Throughout Church history, the Apostles' teachings in the Lord's Church have been and continue to be targeted by Satan and his workers of evil. The purpose of these enemies is to change the righteous character of the Lord's Church that brings glory to God and hope to the lost sinner into an institution that embraces unrighteousness and gives a placebo to the seeker of salvation that will condemn the lost soul forever.

Early Church Fathers

CHAPTER

5

Matthew 7:20

Wherefore by their fruits ye shall know them.

T he close of the written record of the church in the New Testament ends with the Apostle John's revelation on the Island of Patmos, closing the door on biblical history of the first century church. With the end of the recorded biblical history of the conception, birth, empowerment, and development of the Lord's Church, and the arising of the institutions developed to support her as the churches were established, following the history of the church becomes problematic for the next fifteen centuries. We must take into consideration both world history and church tradition, as well as writings from the "Fathers" of the second and third century church to ascertain the development of both the Lord's Church and its alter-ego. A carful observer will find evidence on how the church transforms from the architecture crafted, for the most part, at the hands of the Apostles Paul and Peter as they were guided by God's Holy Spirit. This will be the next phase of our excursion. Examining the development of the Lord's Church in the first few centuries and the continued expansion of the institution that it is housed in will allow a greater understanding of how the Catholic Church came into existence. This same information also will provide evidence how the development of the church and the alter-ego identity was influenced not only by God and the leaders He establishes, but by the influence of false prophets and teachers who took advantage of the institutions to establish a different architecture than was designed by God.

POST-APOSTOLIC LEADERSHIP

After the death of Apostle John, the development of the church was removed from direct apostolic oversite. Most of the teaching of church doctrine was led by second generation Christians and some third generation Christians as well. The canonization of the New Testament scriptures was still in the future of the church. Two centuries would pass before there was general acceptance of what is known now as the contents of the New Testament, and five centuries would pass before the Second Council of Trullan in 692 would provide an official endorsement of what writings would be considered and recognized as the inspired words of God.

The delay from the death of the last Apostle until the Council of Trullan did not open the door for interlopers to add to the New Testament. What was acknowledged as God's inspired revelation had already been generally accepted as what would be later denoted and canonized as the New Testament Bible. We find in the writings of Paul and Peter many references endorsing each other's writings as revelations from God, and in upcoming chapters it is established Irenaeus, a second generation theologian, quotes from the majority of the text that was accepted as canonized scripture at the Council of Trullan.

God had chosen prophets who were empowered by His Holy Spirit and taught by His Son to record His revelation—the record was closed at the death of Apostle John. Many writings were rejected as inspired scripture by the Lord's Church using the standard of the closing of revelation with the death of the Apostle John, they were not rejected on the absence of uniformity with the other accepted writings, but rather they were rejected because God had closed the door for any writings beyond the death of John the Apostle.

The absence of apostolic guidance had a significant impact on both established and new church groups that were being formed. The teachers and leaders of these new church groups often were left with only parts and pieces of the writings of the Apostles and the teachings men had established that parallel the teachings of the Apostles. The absence of authoritative documents to prove or disproved teachings was problematic for the church in the first few centuries. This along with the persecution of the followers of Jesus that often drove new believers from their homes into the "uttermost," provided a fertile ground for the false teachers to plant their seeds of deception in the institutions of the church.

Apostle Paul warned Timothy to be prepared that in the approaching days there would be false prophets and teachers who would assimilate with true believers and endeavor to turn seekers of Jesus away from the truth of God to false doctrines. The unacceptable outcome warned by Apostle Paul was that many would follow their false teaching and would be led from faith in the risen Saviour, as Paul states, "that in the latter times some shall depart from the faith, giving heed to seducing spirits, and doctrines of devils; Speaking lies in hypocrisy; having their conscience seared with a hot iron;" Apostle Peter as well gave ample warning of the danger of false teachers and prophets teaching in the fellowship of the believers in the days ahead. Peter teaches that "...there shall be false teachers among you, who privily shall bring in damnable heresies, even denying the Lord that bought them, and bring upon themselves swift destruction. And many shall follow their pernicious ways; by reason of whom the way of truth shall be evil spoken of. And through covetousness shall they with feigned words make merchandise of you..."

It should come as no surprise that Satan would "salt" the Church of God with false teachers and prophets; deception with part-truths has been his weapon of choice for thousands of years. With Eve it was his weapon when he altered God's word to suggest God was holding back something that would make her godlike. With Jesus, Satan used fragmented scripture to encourage Jesus to short circuit God's plan for the redemption of His creation. In the church, Satan has established and continues to establish false teachers and prophets in the institutions of the church to derail the purpose of the Lord's Church. It is the institution or the alter-ego of the Lord's Church that Satan finds his easiest target to place his workers of evil.

PERSECUTION OF THE LORD'S CHURCH AND HER INSTITUTION

The progress of the church was greatly influenced by the intense persecution of Rome, although the persecution did not occur for religious purposes at first. It is a common held belief that Nero redirected the anger of the disgruntled population of Rome to the Church, assuming the Church would not be able to contest his accusation of their responsibility for the fire in Rome. The first national persecutions of Christians by Rome because of their faith did not occur until the nineties when Domitian became emperor of Rome. The national persecution by Rome combined with the Jews casting Christians out of the Synagogues, using the declaration of the Twelfth Benediction as their authority, made the Lord's Church the object of their persecution. This two-fold attack by Satan against the Lord's Church would influence how and where the Church and her institutions would be established.

The influences of persecution always benefit the Lord's Church, and in times of persecution the faith of believers is strengthened. Persecution also removes much of the need for the institutions of the church, and discourages non-Christians from joining themselves to an institution that is targeted by civil and religious authorities. The desire for power and prestige that many pursue when seeking leadership positions in the institutions of the church, no longer is attractive to weak or unbelieving followers of Christ. When the church is driven underground by persecution, the removal of the opportunity to solicit and gain a favorable response with civil and religious authorities leaves leadership positions to be assumed by committed followers of the Lord Jesus. During times of persecution, the power of the church often is consumed building the hope, faith and purpose of Christians trying to survive the persecution and keep their faith. Persecution drives the followers of Jesus to renew and strengthen their faith in the hope of the Gospel that the outside forces are seeking to undermine and destroy.

The Lord's Church was persecuted but not weakened; the opposition to the Lord's Church   strengthened the faith of the persecuted believers and required the church to depend on and preserve the teachings that were delivered to them by the Apostles. As well, the Church was expunged of the unbelieving followers of the institution built around the Lord's Church. Many people have given their lives for a lie. Many true believers die for the cause of Allah, they will give their lives because they have put their faith and trust in the teachings of Islam. On the other hand, not many are willing to give up wealth, possessions and life for a cause they do not fully trust or embrace. The persecution not only purified the Church but as well removed the false teachers who, as Apostle Peter had said would "make merchandise" of the followers of Jesus.

It was during this time of persecution that the Christian leaders Polycarp of Smyrna and Irenaeus of Antioch lived and served the Lord's Church. Like many others in the history of the Church, they also gave up much for the cause of Christ. Irenaeus and Polycarp left behind letters that give us an indication of the architecture of the church in the second and third century.

POLYCARP AND THE SECOND CENTURY CHURCH

The writings of Polycarp and Irenaeus give us confirmation that the teachings of the apostles were carried forward into the second century church. Polycarp's writings, as well as other historical church documents quoting his teachings, demonstrate his teachings carried the same message of salvation and redemption as were taught by the Apostles. Not one change from the Apostles' teachings can be found in the biblical teachings of Polycarp and Irenaeus. This alone would give evidence that external influences on the church institutions had not altered the doctrine of the Lord's Church and the Holy Spirit was actively guiding His chosen leaders.

From a letter Irenaeus wrote to Florinus, a presbyter at Rome, we can gain insight to how Polycarp influenced Church history. In his letter, Irenaeus said he witnessed the fellowship of Polycarp and early Church leaders in "lower Asia." This meeting had a profound effect on him, and of this occasion Irenaeus said, "I remember the events of that time more clearly than those of recent years... I am able to describe the very place in which the blessed Polycarp sat as he discoursed." He continues to describe this meeting as having a life changing effect on him and his ministry to the Lord. Irenaeus recalls seeing Polycarp fellowship with Apostle John and others who were alive and witnessed and received personally the teachings of Jesus, as he states, "his intercourse with John and with the others who had seen the Lord." Irenaeus continues his memories of Polycarp and gave witness to the validity of Polycarp's endorsement by these who had seen and heard not only the teachings of the Apostles but Jesus Himself. Irenaeus states, "he remembered their words, and what he heard from them concerning the Lord, and concerning His miracles and His teaching, having received them from eyewitnesses of the "Word of life," Polycarp related all things in harmony with the Scriptures."

Polycarp was born in 52 AD and was approved by Apostle John. He bridged the church that was shaped by the Apostles and the Church that would move into the future. Polycarp became the bishop/pastor of Smyrna. From the apostolic anointing by Apostle John, he would lead the Churches of God, in the Asia

Minor area and had great influence over other churches, helping direct and correct the teachings. Polycarp's importance in church history is established in the fact that he is the only church leader who had direct apostolic contact and endorsement as a successor by recognized authorities. Polycarp was martyred in the year 155 AD. His final words, after he was offered to save his life if he would recant his faith, as recorded by Irenaeus were, "Eighty-six years I have served Him, and He has never done wrong. How then, should I be able to blaspheme my King who has saved me?" His prayer gives a reverent insight of God's grace given to the martyr, ". . . In this way and for all things I do praise you, I do bless you, I do glorify you through the eternal and heavenly High Priest, Jesus Christ, your beloved Child: through whom be glory to you with Him and with the Holy Spirit, both now and through ages yet to come. Amen."

IRENAEUS AND THE SECOND AND THIRD CENTURY CHURCH

If Polycarp was the theologian who bridged the church that was shaped by the Apostles into the second century, Irenaeus must be considered as the theologian that shepherded the Lord's Church into the third century. He has been called the most important Christian theologian between the apostles and the third century.

Irenaeus was a Greek from Asia, today southwestern Turkey, born probably between 130-140 AD and like Timothy was born to a God-fearing home. As previously discussed, Irenaeus witnessed Polycarp's approval by Apostle John and other elders taught by Jesus. The Holy Spirit allowed him to observe not only the teachings of Polycarp, but to witness Polycarp being taught by Apostle John. Irenaeus from his own testimony said these events were burned into his memory. The Holy Spirit was preparing this young man for the important role he would have in the forming of the Lord's Church. The first time the word "Christian" is found in any known documents outside of the Bible is when Irenaeus uses the word to describe a true follower of Jesus.

Irenaeus would become a missionary to the Celts and eventually an elder in the Lyons congregation. Irenaeus was later to be ordained the second Pastor of the church in Lyons. When the heresies of Gnosticism and other false teachings were taking hold of the church in Rome, Irenaeus composed what is known as Adversus Haereses (Against Heresies) exposing teachings that were providing confusion of true Christian doctrine.

Irenaeus exposed many false teachers by name and many heresies taking root in the churches of Rome. In the exposure of the Valentinians (followers and teachers of Gnosticism) as false teachers, Irenaeus set a standard for examining the teachings to be endorsed and allowed in the church, "Such, then, is their system, which neither the prophets announced, nor the Lord taught, nor the apostles delivered, but of which they boast that beyond all others they have a perfect knowledge. They gather their views from other sources than the Scriptures."

In this statement Irenaeus set the standards that should be referenced to endorse any teacher or teaching in the churches institutions. The standard for sound doctrine and acceptable teaching in the second and third century church and likewise today's assemblies should consist of; the teachings of the prophets, when about and for the Lord and His Church they spoke (both Old and New Testament), the teachings of Jesus and the teachings of the Apostles. All non-scriptural sources and any teaching that includes, "perfect Knowledge," were to be rejected and exposed by men of God to protect the church from evil practices.

Irenaeus recognized that as the institutions of the churches are established there will soon be the producing of documents and "statements of faith" as the institution defines its position on God, Christ, The Holy Spirit, salvation, scripture. Further, they will define how and when church action and ordinances are to be observed, requirements to be in good standing with the institution, how the institution will govern the control the operation of the institution, and how institutional polity will be established. Irenaeus well observed as the institution establishes its identity, often denominational or church elders' writings, will be given as references for the creation of its ideology and practices. If these references are established and validated in the scripture, there is no issue. When the references leverage scripture to conclusions that are not supported by or are not consistent with the scripture as afore enumerated, heresy is the outcome and must be confronted by exposing the conflict with God's Word.

IRENAEUS AND THE CATHOLIC CHURCH

The Catholic Church embraces Irenaeus as supporter and promoter of the Catholic Church, and additionally established him as a "Saint." The Catholic Church claims his statement defending the singularity of teachings as evidence of only one true institution for the church to be hosted in. Irenaeus' proclamation recorded in his writing "Against Heresies" is offered as evidence of their claim. The statement made by Irenaeus, the Catholic Church claims, is evidence supporting a single institutional authority, based on this statement, "and maintained that the bishops in different cities are known as far back as the Apostles and that the bishops provided the only safe guide to the interpretation of Scripture."

In addition, the Catholic Church claims Irenaeus was supporting a singular church institution when he wrote a letter correcting the church in Smyrna. This letter contained a warning of similar institutional failure as addressed by the Apostle Paul's warning to the Church of Corinth's misuse of church ordinances. Irenaeus, responding to the abuse of the ordinances, wrote there were, "divisions, as being the beginning of evils." The practices of their "love feasts" or Lord's Supper as well as the baptism of new converts were being practiced without spiritual oversite and was degrading the purpose of these events.

Irenaeus said that pastoral approval was required for these events to take place. He states, "Do ye all follow the bishop, as Jesus Christ doth the Father; and follow the presbyters as the apostles; and have respect unto the deacons as unto the commandment of God. Let no one, apart from the bishop, do any of the things that appertain unto the church. Let that Eucharist (the Lord's Supper) alone be considered valid which is celebrated in the presence of the bishop, or of him to whom he shall have entrusted it. Wherever the bishop appear, there let the multitude be; even as wherever Christ Jesus is, there is the catholic [*meaning "comprehensive" or "universal" and not speaking to the yet to be established institution*] church. It is not lawful either to baptize, or to hold a love-feast without the consent of the bishop; but whatsoever he shall approve of, that also is well pleasing unto God, to the end that whatever is done may be safe and sure."

It is noteworthy to ascertain in this statement the biblical word bishop can and is interchangeably used as bishop, pastor, and under-shepherd in the New Testament. Irenaeus never endorsed any single church identity or any church sacrament to have control over the eternal destination of souls or how the churches were structure as local assemblies of believers. His warning was to protect the integrity of not only these ordinances but to preserve purity of the doctrines taught and practiced by the different churches. The Catholic Church's view on the "sacraments" of baptism and communion contributing to the salvation of the sinner was not in this writing or any other by Irenaeus; only the completed work of Jesus is considered as a theology of soteriology. Most traditional churches practice this same standard today, with the appointed elder ensuring the proper discharge of these ordinances of the church.

In one of Irenaeus' writings discovered in 1904, *The Demonstration of the Apostolic Preaching*, he dispels any connection to the Catholic Church. In this book he clearly identifies that the message that the church should proclaim is a relationship with God that is forged by a personal encounter with Jesus and is the work of the Holy Spirit independent of any earth-bound Church relationship. While Irenaeus taught a consistency of doctrine from the Apostles to his current position in Lyons, he never embraced a universal or Catholic Church structure.

Irenaeus' closest contact with the Apostles was Polycarp. Correspondingly, he gave special consideration to the succession of teaching passed from the Apostles to Polycarp, from Polycarp to himself, and then to the overseers in the church and the teachers who were taught and discipled by himself. In his teachings, Irenaeus gives us evidence of a conduit of truth—the doctrines of the second and third century church were the same doctrines of the Apostles. The teachings accepted into today's church should be validated in the teachings found in the New Testament.

The importance held by Irenaeus in shepherding the church out of the second century into the third century cannot be overstated. Irenaeus' writings are identical to the Canon that became accepted as New Testament scripture. He quotes from most of its writings, though he doesn't quote Philemon, James, 2 Peter or 3 John, it can be assumed he did not have copies of these manuscripts. As well Irenaeus acknowledged all the Gospels as authentic.

PROPERTY AND ASSETS

It was the practice of the first and second Century churches to meet in homes and public places, and this practice continued for most of the second and third century churches. Constantine recognized Christianity as a legal state religion in 313 AD, and would change not only the meeting place of the church, but will give birth to a new church institution in which the Lord's Church would soon not be welcomed.

Until this radical change in the church's identity, the only church owned building that can be identified was a short lived attempt in Dura Europos on the Euphrates River in eastern Roman Syria. It was a house that was remodeled in the mid-third century. Two rooms were combined to form the assembly room, and another room became a baptistry. History records it was destroyed a few years later by the Persians.

Unequally Yoked, the Unholy Union of Church and state

Matthew 23:9-10
And call no man your father upon the earth: for one is your Father, which is in heaven. Neither be ye called masters: for one is your Master, even Christ.

A s we move from the second century into the third century, the last direct connection with the Apostles comes to an end. Polycarp who was discipled by Apostle John, and Irenaeus who had witnessed Polycarp with Apostle John and others who had walked with Jesus, now are in glory. The third century church was a difficult time for the developing church. For the most part, the history of the church is found in the Apostle Paul's "Gentile" church.

As the Gospel moved from the Asian provinces to the "utter most part of the world," false teachers and prophets in Rome had fulfilled the words of warning by Apostles Paul and Peter. Gnostics and a multitude of false teachers had "crept in" to the institutions of the Lord's Church. The institution of the Church of Rome had adopted many of the false teachings Irenaeus had warned would undermine the intent and purpose of the Lord's Church. The change in doctrine allowed the culture and practices of heathenism to be adopted and practiced by the Church in Rome.

ANOTHER GOSPEL

The development of the structure of the institution in Rome would create what is now known as the Roman Catholic Church, which has a long and shady history. The Catholic Church makes many statements about how it came into existence. Its view of history is not based in fact, nor will it stand up to biblical or historical scrutiny. The idea of a single, supreme church leader called a pope did not exist for many centuries of church history. In fact, the pastors or bishops of churches in the first centuries often were called pope as a term of endearment and respect, as the word pope simply means *father* or *papa*.

The Catholic Church's claim that Jesus left His Kingdom in Heaven, lived a life of sinless perfection, died on Golgotha, conquered death in His rising from the grave, and returned to His Kingdom with His father, all to establish the authority of the institution of the Catholic Church to have authority over all matters of man's relationship with God is not only false, it is heresy. For the institution in Rome to claim that the purpose of the sacrifice, suffering, and death of the Apostles was to produce this Catholic system of institutional authority is not supported by scripture. Furthermore, it violates every possible teaching found in the Bible and disgraces the work and lives of the Great Men of God.

When Peter said to Jesus, "we have forsaken all, and followed thee; what shall we have therefore?" How would Peter respond if Jesus had answered, "Peter, you will give all you have including your life to establish an institution based in Rome that will be populated by evil men who will take the lives of millions of people to establish and enforce its power over people groups, church groups and civil governments." Would Peter have been eager to have this as his legacy of what Jesus did with him and through him?

Most of the teachings of the Catholic Church violates Irenaeus' *The Demonstration of the Apostolic Preaching*. The support for a universal authority for all followers of Jesus cannot be supported without referencing "special knowledge" Irenaeus warned was false teachings. Most of the teachings of the Catholic Church are rooted in Paganism. It is beyond the scope of this book to debunk the many false teaching and practices of the Catholic Church, but it should be stated as fact: *if the teachings of the Catholic Church is all a lost soul hears they will be secluded from the soul-saving preaching of the Gospel.* The Gospel that is presented by the Catholic Church is without a doubt "another gospel" the Apostle Paul warned is "accursed."

THE FIRST "POPE" OF ROME

The claim that Simon Peter was the first Pope of the Roman Catholic Church is unfounded by secular or church history. There is no evidence that Peter ever made a journey to Rome. In fact, the only historical reference to Peter and his affiliation with the Church in Rome is when Irenaeus places Paul and Peter in the conversations of the Church in Rome. This statement was reflecting oral history that was not supported in biblical or secular history, and there is a better explanation of the "Peter in Rome" that will be discussed later. The fact that Paul was declared the Apostle to the Gentiles and Peter was the Apostle to the Jews gives clear understanding that God established two distinct and different church identities; for Peter to wander off to Rome and establish a church would violate this understanding and agreement. Most assuredly, the outcome would have caused Apostle Paul to once again confront Peter as he did in Antioch when he was out of line with the teachings of God.

Many believe there was another Simon in Rome at this same time, and that he was the source of much of the false teachings that were gaining traction in the church at Rome. Dr. Luke introduces us to a Simon in Acts chapter 8. This Simon was a practitioner of the dark arts and had the capability to lead people to treat him as a "great one," or Simon Magus. The people in Samaria gave him credit of having his power from God, and Simon had a "church" or following of people. When Philip came to Samaria, Simon's "church" heard the Gospel of Jesus and many hearing Philip preach the Gospel believed and were saved. When Simon saw his "church" dissimulate with Philip, he also followed and was baptized. When Apostle Peter comes to see the events taking place in Samaria, the followers of Jesus in Samaria were infilled with the Holy Spirit and had a visual (just as on Pentecost in Jerusalem) entrance into the Lord's Church. Simon's false conversion did not warrant an infilling of the Holy Spirit, and when he tried to procure it with money he was rebuked by Peter, as it is recorded, "Thou hast neither part nor lot in this matter: for thy heart is not right in the sight of God."

Simon considered himself a Christian and Peter's reprimand about his ill begot desire to have power; power that was God-given, not given by the practice of the dark arts, did not change his mind. Even though Simon was not born again, he did not reject the teachings of the Gospel, he was unwilling to reject his apostate view of having power from the Gospel. When he was reprimanded by Peter he said, "Pray ye to the Lord for me, that none of these things which ye have spoken come upon me."

Many historians support this conclusion. It is clear from Simon's response to Peter he did not reject all the teachings of the Apostles, they were just added to the mix of his Paganism he already taught and embraced. A new Gospel came from this co-mingling of truth and lies; Satan's choice of weapon that has proved effective throughout human history.

Church history identifies Simon Magus as a promoter of a mixture of Paganism coupled with Jewish traditions and customs along with Christian teachings to form a counterfeit Gospel. The merging of the Pagan belief system with the traditions and legalism of Judaism mixed in with the supernatural aspect of Christianity allowed Simon Magus to build a "universal" teaching that would be inclusive of most all people groups. Historian Justin Martyr describes Simon Magus as a Christian who came to Rome, established the heretical teachings of his corrupted Gospel and was a teacher with many followers. The teachings of Simon Magus *could* have been the corrupt Gospel in Rome Irenaeus identified and rebuked as false and destructive to Christianity, and *could* have also been the motivation of his writing, *The Demonstration of the Apostolic Preaching.*

Is it possible Simon Magus is the Simon Peter that the Catholic Church claims as the first Pope of their form of Christianity? The evidence supporting Simon Magus as the first Pope Magus of the Catholic Church has more biblical and historical evidence than the fabricated and shady history that is presented as fact by the Catholic historians.

Establishing how the Catholic Church was founded is a straightforward path to follow in secular historical documents. The Edict of Toleration was written by Caesar Galerius, and was issued by the Roman Emperor Diocletian in AD 305. This soon became Roman law, officially ending the persecution of Christianity, and thereby allowing for the church in Rome to come out of the shadows that persecution had demanded for its continued existence.

The Roman Government galvanized their popular support by promoting the "Imperial Cult," a forced worship of the current emperor and his family as gods. Citizens of Rome were forced to pledge allegiance to the emperor, and rejection was a sentence of death. Christians were often the target of the Emperor's wrath for the unwillingness to acknowledge the "god" status of the Emperor. Emperors often built popular support by unleashing the masses to confiscate property, wealth, and often lives of followers of Christ. The Edict of Toleration established Christian worship as legitimate and acknowledged by the Roman Empire. In part, the decree stated, "Wherefore, for this our indulgence, they ought to pray to their God for our safety, for that of the republic, and for their own, that the commonwealth may continue uninjured on every side, and that they may be able to live securely in their homes." Property was to be restored with the Roman Government paying any compensation required for the reclaiming of the property by the Christian, as the Edict of Milan states, "...the same shall be restored to the Christians without payment or any claim of recompense and without any kind of fraud or deception." Christianity was now treated like all the Pagan religions in Rome.

Just a few years later in AD 313, Western Roman Emperor Constantine endorsed and adopted the Galerius decree. Constantine, it is said, converted to Christianity during a war against Maxentius his brother-in-law before the battle. It is recorded Constantine was convinced that he needed celestial support. While he was waiting for the beginning of the battle, he saw a flaming cross, and written underneath, "in this sign you will be victorious," he took this as a sign he was to become a Christian. Constantine is recorded as refusing baptism until his death bed in fear he would sin and lose all hope of redemption. Constantine believed that the church and the government of Rome should be as close in identity as possible, as a result Constantine declared Sunday an official Roman holiday and made churches tax-exempt. The protected status and the ability to own tax exempt assets was the birth of the institution of the Catholic Church of Rome, and the ensuing political structure that would establish the first *Pontifex Maximus* (literally "greatest pontiff"). This would be a blatant shift in how the institutions of the church in the first through third century were organized and housed in homes.

It was under Constantine's rule Pagan worship was officially merged in the doctrines of the Church in Rome. Constantine established December 25, the birthday of the Pagan Sun god, as the official birthday celebration of Jesus's birth. A special day of worship would be set aside and was declared a holyday. We now call this day Christmas; its name is derived from the Catholic's special mass for Jesus' birthday called "Christ's Mass."

It was only a century before, Irenaeus, along with other elders, waged and lost a spiritual battle against the Church at Rome when they changed the traditional Passover observance to "Easter." Changing the purpose of the holyday from the death of

Jesus to his resurrection was a departure from any known celebration by the church, and it is further probable Constantine officially established the Easter observance on a day when a vile and Pagan Goddess of Ashtoreth (known by many other names) is celebrated in pagan worship. As well, Constantine most likely established the Catholic holyday Lent, based on the worship of the pagan goddess Ishtar son's Tammuz's death and resurrection.

Constantine's marriage of the church and civil government allowed for the church's institution to amass significant amounts of assets and possessions. The wealth of the Church in Rome allowed for prestige and power—not just for the institution itself, but also to be transferred to the ones controlling the wealth.

PAPAL SUCCESSION

The Church of Rome's unsubstantiated claim of Papal succession back to Apostle Peter is false. The High worship leader of Roman paganism was the Pontifex Maximus or Supreme Pontiff. In the afore described relation of the Imperial Cult, this position was held by the current Emperor of Rome and the Pontifex Maximus by default was the final authority over all of Rome's temple worship. It can be argued that Constantine's direct over sight of church affairs, his institution of Lent, Easter and Christmas as official holydays of the church in Rome, and the merging of Christianity with paganism established him as the first Pontifex Maximus of the Roman Catholic Church.

There was no fixed process for papal replacement until the middle of the eleventh century. In the fourth and fifth centuries, Bishops for the Roman Church, for the most part, were selected by the pope vacating the position, or national rulers appointing the pope. The wealth the church had amassed was the motiva-tion for replacing leadership. Succession of the leaders of Rome's church were chosen primarily out of the "inner-circle" to allow for the control of the assets. This era was filled with violent take-overs and political deceit for the coveted position. The battles of papal succession were often held out of the view of the public, and for a while an external facade was made to give appearance the laity was a part of the selection.

The seventh century found the institution of the church in Rome evolving from housing the Lord's Church where the Gos-pel was preached, to a political financial power house; and it is to this very day. The protection of the Roman church and its as-sets provided by Constantine's merging of the church with the civil governments allowed the church to become a powerful and dominant institution. Understanding the power and wealth held by the church, the Emperors limited the selection of the church leaders to clerics and aristocrats, and began to sell the positions in the church. This practice was to become known as simony. The origin of the word simony has an interesting history; it is de-rived from a Latin Middle English word *simonie*. Simony originat-ed in the twelfth century from Simon Magus, who, as mentioned earlier, attempted to purchase apostolic powers. This is perhaps more ancillary information that Simon Magus was the "Simon" the Catholics place as the first pope of the Roman Church.

By the tenth century, bishops were medieval lords that re-tained armed forces which fought among themselves for the wealth of the lands they were granted authority to control. Si-mony had changed not only the purpose of the institution of the church, but the identity was changed from a place that God's people assembled to a dwelling place of evil. The Council of Cardinals was created in 1059 to elect the pope of Rome. This is the system used today for papal succession.

The evil that was practiced by the Church of Rome had no limits. The Catholic Church launched a war to destroy everyone who opposed the establishment of universal church authority, a movement called *The Inquisitions*. The Inquisitions began in the late twelfth century and ended in 1834 with official end of the Spanish Inquisition. How much wealth was confiscated and how many lives were taken is not known, although some estimate fifty million people were tortured and murdered during this time. Today, the Roman Catholic Church is still a powerful political machine. They are the only religious body to have diplomatic representation to the nations, and in Villa Domiziana, America funds an embassy and ambassador to the Roman Catholic Church. Clearly, the political view of the separation of church and state did not apply here.

CHRISTIANITY AND THE FALL OF ROME

The effect on world history regarding Constantine's vision of the flaming cross in the sky would not be trivial or anecdotal. His vision would have a significant effect in shaping world and Christian history. Constantine's vision would change not only the future of Rome, but would be responsible for the development of a malevolent Christian church institution. This institution would not just become a power to influence civil governments but would as well become the enemy of the Lord's Church. As the Roman Church set out to establish its power over the masses of people, it would identify, reject, and condemn any other Christian group and seek to end their influence by any and all means. The vision with the associated message that compelled Constantine to embrace Christianity would also persuade him to align the entire Roman Empire with the Roman Church, not Christianity, in a universal understanding.

Constantine was not just in pursuit of his perceived need for a personal response to his vision but he was persuaded that Rome was to embrace a national conversion to Christianity. Constantine believed this personal and national response to his vision would allow him not only to win the battle against his brother-in-law Maxentius, who was challenging Constantine's attempt to unify the Roman Empire, but also would secure a unified Empire that would be under his control. The unification of Rome with Christianity would not prove to be the power to hold the Empire together but would play a substantial roll in the demise of the Roman Empire less than a century later.

The Roman Empire's adoption and advancement of this new religion, Christianity, was not only accepted by Constantine but its national success was personally superintended and established at the will and political supremacy of Constantine.

The best treatment a Christian could expect before the Edict of Toleration was to face discrimination for the simple practice of their faith, regardless if their faith was exercised in public or in the privacy of their homes. Often this discrimination against Christians living in areas under Roman control escalated and led to persecution by both civil and religious authorities. This persecution would force Christians out of their homes with the confiscation of their property and often ended in death or worse; death in the Coliseum as entertainment for the citizens of Rome who enjoyed battles fought to the death as a way to satisfy their blood lust.

In the beginning of the fourth century, Christianity was a marginalized underground religion in the Roman Empire and the Christian faith was hidden from the general population by necessity. When Christianity was exposed to the general population or the civil government, it was forced back into the shadows of society by its enemies. To be a Christian in this age was to live under a verdict of guilty without the benefit of adjudication. The Christian persecution that started under Emperor Nero after the great fire of Rome in 64 AD started an organized persecution by the Roman government that continued through Emperor Domitian in 96 AD. The Christian persecution culminated under Emperor Diocletian, who issued four edicts relating to the Christian community.

Diocletian's first edict was an order to destroy any and all church property and to have all its treasures seized. All Christian scriptures were ordered destroyed along with any other Christian documents found. This decree also established as illegal any public or private assembling of Christians. Christians were denied their privileges of citizenship, along with the right to petition the courts, resulting in the loss of defense for anyone accused of any crime and making them subject to any and all torture any civil authority wished to impose. Followers of Christ, along with the leaders of the church groups, were to be publicly humiliated and along with all other Christians denied legal standing and subject to torture and denied their freedom. Christian civil leaders along with soldiers were deprived of their positions, rank and privileges, and freed men were enslaved once again. Under the order of Galerius, any resisting this edict were to be sacrificed by burning alive.

Diocletian's second edict was not anything new, but reinforced and expedited his desire to destroy the Lord's Church. The edict's persecution was in particular directed against church leaders. Some historians suggest the second edict was given to ensure the removal of Christian leaders from the people to suppress the continued growth of the Lord's Church in spite of his first edict. History records the prisons began to fill beyond capacity as the edict was executed across the empire. Prisons were filled with deacons, preachers and bishops. History records that the prisons were so filled with Christians that criminals were released to make room to accommodate the second edict of Diocletian.

Diocletian's third edict was issued for his twentieth year celebration as emperor of Rome. This edict would give amnesty to any church leader arrested under the first and second edict and would allow them their freedom if they would make a sacrifice to the gods of Rome. Many believe in his attempt to end Christianity, Diocletian had galvanized the gospel in the Christian community and had advanced the proclaiming of the Gospel of Jesus. The third edict was an attempt to fracture the Christian community with apostate Christian leaders.

Diocletian's demands for the most part fell on deaf ears. There was some insignificant shift in the Christian community as many of the church leaders were made to worship the gods of Rome but do so under the distress of pain and torture and when they were released returned to their ministry to God. Many civil leaders in an attempt to empty the prisons of innocent Christians many were released after they were told they had sacrificed to the gods of Rome when in fact they had not.

Diocletian's forth edict was issued in response to the failure of his first three edicts attempt to end Christianity. His final edict was an attempt to identify and destroy anyone who would not deny their faith in Christ. This edict would require all people, men, women and children to be gathered in a public forum and require them to make a sacrifice to the gods of Rome—if they refused, they were to be executed.

After three centuries of persecution it is easy to see how Christians in this age could look at Constantine with hope and embrace the nationalization of Christianity. The results would not be long felt. Soon the Church of Rome would pick up the mantel of persecution to target any follower of Jesus that would not accept the Roman Catholic Church as the only and final authority concerning Christianity.

Under the supervision of Constantine, Christianity in less than a century would move from the shadows of Roman society and become an official religion accepted and practiced by most of the Roman Empire. This is not to be understood that Rome as a nation abandoned the practice of pagan religious worship, but rather Constantine legitimized Christianity as a state approved religious exercise. It was accepted as a part of the fabric of Rome's religious practice and was added into the collection of the many pagan gods revered by the Romans.

The Roman Catholic Church secures its future after the fall of the Roman Empire.

Constantine's vision and his ensuing action would insure the Roman Church would be positioned as a wealthy and politically empowered institution in the centuries following the collapse of the Roman Empire that became known as the Dark Ages. It was under the guidance and protection of Constantine the Church of Rome developed its power base with both the politically elite and the masses of common people that would secure its survival in the social political chaos, often referred to as the Dark Ages. This chaos would begin with the collapse of the Roman Empire and would last for six centuries until Pope Leo III established a church-state relationship with Charlemagne. Historians commonly agree the Dark Ages ended when Charlemagne was crowned emperor of the Romans in the late ninth century by the Roman Catholic Church.

Constantine's expansion of the Roman Catholic Church would establish the Roman Church as a powerful political and religious institution that would be able to solidify its position of power not only over Rome but over most of the known world in less than a century. Constantine's proclamation and promotion of the Edict of Toleration which stated that "it was proper that the Christians and all others should have liberty to follow that mode of religion which to each of them appeared best," was not just granting tolerance to all religions, including Christianity but was the first step of many that would establish the Roman Catholic Church as a political power. The union of the Roman Catholic Church with the Roman Empire came with an associated cost of the weakening and the suppression of the Lord's Church as the Roman Church's institution gained power and wealth.

The Edict of Milan was the second major change in the Roman government's position on Christianity that had even a greater impact than the earlier Edict of Toleration, in that it returned the confiscated property of persecuted Christians. The wealth that had been confiscated from Christian families for centuries was returned not to the families, but to the Roman Catholic Church.

The Toleration edict made the empire on the surface appear impartial with regard to religious worship but the Edict of Milan empowered the Roman Church with wealth that could change

Unequally Yoked, the Unholy Union of Church and State

not the hearts of men, but their political allegiance. Constantine's true intent concerning the Roman Church would be revealed in his establishment and promotion of Christianity in the last years of his life.

Constantine viewed himself as the not only the patron of the Roman Catholic Church but also as its protector. Constantine as Emperor used the wealth of Rome to support and build the Roman Catholic Church. He had a large number of cathedrals built at Rome's expense and gave the Roman Church many privileges among which was to be exempt from taxes, not just the church but the clergy as well. This benefit was promoted to high ranking officers with their conversion to the Church. In doing so, they would be established in clergy positions in the church giving them like privileges possessed by the leadership positions in the church if they supported Constantine's efforts to establish the Roman Catholic Church. Along with the returned wealth that was confiscated, Constantine also endowed the church with land and much wealth.

Constantine built a new imperial capital he named Constantinople. Rome had for centuries celebrated its inclusiveness of all religions and had been established on polytheism. The single greatest landmark that gave Rome its identity was the Pantheon. Although the Pantheon became a Catholic church in the seventh century, it was first built as a temple to all gods. Pantheon is a Greek word meaning "honor all Gods." In fact, the Pantheon was built for a celebration of Rome's polytheism.

Constantine continued to establish the Church of Rome as a national religion and powerful institution when he began to employ overtly Christian architecture. He built churches within the city walls and did not accommodate vestiges of polytheism—no

90

temples from other religions were allowed in Constantine's new capital of Rome, Constantinople.

He also required those who had not converted to Christianity to pay for the new city. He used this financial tool not so much to fund the building of his Christian city, but as an evangelistic tool to compel people to convert to Christianity, thereby preserving their wealth.

This mandate led to the loss of support and funding of the temples in Rome. They were soon converted into church buildings, and as a result, wealth was flowing to the imperial treasure to build the Christian City of Constantinople. Constantine did not need to use force to implement the eradication of polytheism in Rome. He used the power of preservation of personal wealth to persuade Rome's citizens to reject polytheism and to encourage the national acceptance of the Roman Catholic Church.

Constantine also granted imperial favor to the Roman Church, and new opportunities were opened to members of this church group, including the right to compete with other Romans for high government positions. As a result, Christians gained greater acceptance into civil and governmental social order. Men who refused to convert to Christianity were denied positions of power in his Government, giving the Church even greater control.

The religious and political fabric of Rome before Constantine was framed by the practice of many pagan religions adopting from their many conquests. These religions were collected and established as legitimate religious practices, and were recognized and authorized by the Roman empirical government. All of the pagan religions embraced polytheism, providing not only unity among themselves but as well promoted the Roman's promotion of the Imperial Cult in that the Emperor himself was a god and was to be worshiped.

The practice of "Emperor Worship" held an important facet in keeping Rome unified into one empire. Christianity teaches, affirms, and believes in the singleness of God as embodied in the Trinity of God the Father, Jesus the Son and the Holy Spirit. Christians are monotheistic and this ran counter to the traditional polytheistic Roman religion. Christians were unable to embrace the worship of the gods of Rome, or to worship the Emperor as god. The exclusivity of Christianity and the rejection of polytheism has been and will be rejected by the world, and is what made the Lord's church a target of the Roman Government and a target of the civil authorities today.

Constantine's promotion of the Roman Catholic Church would soon displace the polytheistic Roman religions including the worship of the emperor of Rome as god. This Roman twist in polytheism that allowed the emperor to ascent to a celestial status, and provided an opportunity for the different cultures to co-exist and worship a sole national deity would soon come to an end.

The increasing power the Roman Catholic Church exercised in the political domain of Rome did not singularly cause the decline and fall of the Roman Empire, but many historians argue that the rise of the influence of the Roman Catholic Church was certain to have contributed to the empire's decline and fall.

The polytheistic teachings of the Catholic Church would soon engage the empire in a massive political change. The eroding of the entrenched polytheism of traditional Roman values brought to an end what had been the capacity that provided the ability to absorb the cultures from the various conquered nations into the empire.

ROME ESTABLISHES THE ONLY ACCEPTED CHURCH

The Edict of Thessalonica was jointly issued by Theodosius I, Gratian, and Valentinian II on 27 February 380 AD. By edict, Rome commanded everyone to be a Christian. Not just convert to Christianity, but to accept the Roman Catholic Church as the only true church. A Catholic Christian, was one who held as true the Nicene Creed. The following year, 381 AD, Theodosius issued another edict specifically requiring worship of the one God according to the Nicene Creed.

The Nicene Creed states:

I believe in one God, Father Almighty, Creator of
heaven and earth, and of all things visible and invisible.

And in one Lord Jesus Christ, the only-begotten Son of
God, begotten of the Father before all ages;

Light of Light, true God of true God, begotten,
not created, of one essence with the Father
through Whom all things were made.

Who for us men and for our salvation
came down from heaven and was incarnate
of the Holy Spirit and the Virgin Mary and became man.

He was crucified for us under Pontius Pilate,
and suffered and was buried;

And He rose on the third day,
according to the Scriptures.

He ascended into heaven
and is seated at the right hand of the Father;

And He will come again with glory to judge the living
and dead. His kingdom shall have no end.

And in the Holy Spirit, the Lord, the Creator of life,
Who proceeds from the Father, Who together with the
Father and the Son is worshipped and glorified, Who
spoke through the prophets.

In one, holy, catholic, and apostolic Church.

I confess one baptism for the forgiveness of sins.

I look for the resurrection of the dead,
and the life of the age to come.

These edicts made orthodox Catholic Christianity the only accepted form of Christianity, and any other faction or practice was suppressed by the church and civil authorities. The outcome of this edict was the persecution of anyone professing themselves Christians outside not just The Nicene Creed, but the understanding of the Roman Catholic Church. This persecution was extended to include pagans, and people of the Jewish faith.

Tracking the influence and development of the church's institution becomes problematic in the years following the collapse of the Roman Empire. The Dark Ages is generally accepted to have started in the late forth and early fifth century with the collapse of Rome, and came to an end at the rise of the rule of Charlemagne also known as Charles the Great in the late eighth century.

The Dark Ages is associated with a religious struggle authored by the Roman Catholic Church. Christians who rejected the doctrine and power the Catholic Church held over the spiritual and physical lives of believers became objects of the Catholic Church's wrath. Without the structure of civil law, the Catholic Church became a law unto themselves and had no reservations on how to place the known world in subject to the Pope and the Church he ruled over.

The Catholic Church does not view this time as "dark" but rather Catholic history records this as the period of consolidation of power in the battle to control the development of the Church and to establish their place in history as the sole "Catholic" church, and to become a world power in the exercise of religious and political power. It is during the Dark Ages much of the theology and structure of the Catholic Church is formed.

The priesthood and the creation of a single authority vested in the position of the Pope came about during this period. In the six centuries following the creation of the Roman Catholic Church, there was no central appointment of the papacy. There were often men simultaneous holding the position of the Pope. There was no permanent process for papal choice before 1059 AD. Often this position was filled by the previous Popes, the bishops of Rome and the leaders of the Catholic Church selecting his replacement. Simony, the purchase of position by money, was a means to the position the king used as well in appointment business—King Henry III installed three popes into their office in a six-year period.

The Catholic Church after the end of the Dark Ages would for the next six hundred years rule as a threat and persecutor of the Lord's Church and to non-Catholics across the world. Christians who resisted the Catholic Church's institution in its attempt to establish themselves as the single and sole authority in the spiritual and eternal destiny in the lives would pay a high price, that of forfeiture of possessions and often their lives. The survivors who oppose the power of the Catholic Church observed the Dark Ages and the next six centuries as a period of Catholic exploitation of the cause of Christ.

The followers of Jesus rejected and still reject the papal doctrines and the hierarchy of the priesthood established in institution of the Catholic Church during this age. The sole purpose of the creation of Catholic doctrines on soteriology and the structure of the priesthood was to establish power that was imposed on the masses of people. This power was exercised to control people with the intended outcome of amassing wealth for the church and its leaders, and granting power to control civil governments.

When the Roman Government collapsed, there was no longer a centralized civil authority to control the evil men who were in power of the Catholic Church. The vacuum of civil authority in the dark ages provided the political and cultural environment that would allow for the resident evil in this institution to have limitless progress. Without the restraining hand of civil government, evil institutions and men will seek to enlarge themselves as much as possible.

God gives government to provide a collective conscience when individual conscience fails. We are instructed on the importance of civil government in I Peter, "Submit yourselves to every ordinance of man for the Lord's sake: whether it be to the king, as supreme; Or unto governors, as unto them that are sent by him for the punishment of evildoers..."

Many today seek a political landscape limited or void of any civil authority. For the most part, the people are involved in activities that God's word or common law would find unacceptable. On the other side of this issue we find people who want to establish a Theocracy where God's word would control all human activity. The problem with either position is human involvement. Mankind is fallen and corrupt. God established mankind that cannot rule themselves because of their failed conscience, and a collective conscience is established to help insure limits on the evil of any single person. A collective conscience of civil government in spite of its corruption is better to rule over the civil behavior than a single corrupt person.

The writer of Hebrews notes the problems associated with a single authority in spiritual affairs when it is noted, "And they truly were many priests, because they were not suffered to continue by reason of death." Men rise and fall in power and in longevity. Without the establishment of civil government, a single man will assume absolute power and as it is well known, power breads corruption and absolute power allows for absolute corruption.

Corruption was the outcome of the Dark Ages. The institution of the Catholic Church structured itself with a single office of a "High Priest." The man who would have the title of Pope would be a supreme ruler over all of humanity. The Catholic Church during the Dark Ages and the centuries to come established themselves as the only source for spiritual and political justice, and became absolutely corrupt.

The Dark Ages ended with the re-establishing of a unified civil government. For the first time after the fall of Rome as a world power, there was a national attempt to unify multiple people groups into a single kingdom. Charlemagne, who became king of the Franks, was determined to recreate a single world power in the same configuration of the Romans. Charlemagne set out to unite all Germanic peoples into one kingdom this would include modern time peoples that would include the Afrikaners, Austrians, Danes, Dutch, English, Flemish, Frisians, Germans, Icelanders, Lowland Scots, Norwegians, Swedes and others (including displaced populations, such as most European Americans). The Roman Catholic Church recognized the power and the potential of a church state relationship with Charlemagne. Pope Leo III crowned Charlemagne emperor of the Romans in the late ninth century. This move would ensure the survival of the power of the Roman Catholic Church would have in world affairs for many centuries. Charlemagne, like the Roman Emperor Constance, used the churches institution to convert his subjects to Christianity.

The Protest/The Love of Money is the Root of All Evil

Ecclesiastes 5:13

Here is a sore evil which I have seen under the sun, namely, riches kept for the owners thereof to their hurt.

The institution of the Catholic Church was expanding its power and control over civil governments and the masses of people. The union of the civil government with the Catholic Church established by Constantine in 313 AD soon led to the pagans' property, temples and wealth to be transferred to the Catholic institution. The power and prestige of the Catholic institution was established in the large and lavish compounds confiscated from the pagans and later built by powerful church leaders.

The growing institution demanded more wealth to fund its growth and turned to the non-Catholic people groups as a revenue stream by labeling them heretics. The Roman Church moved to suppress and destroy the "heretics," but the underlying reason for the attacks was to gain their property and wealth for the advancement of the power and prestige of the institution. Inquisitions against the "heretics" to gain wealth was a practice of the Catholic institution until the end of the Spanish Inquisition in the1800's. The revenue from the inquisitions was not enough to satisfy the Roman Church, so they turned to the masses to gain the wealth they desired often on the backs of the poor.

FALSE DOCTRINES AND LIES

The establishment of indulgences was unjustly used by the Catholic Church to gain treasure and power on the backs of the masses of people. This was an evil of such proportions, the Roman Catholic Church had reached an unsustainable level. Evil always has a breaking point when it implodes of its own weight of sin, or God responds to the evil. In the garden, God intervened with a promised future redemption of mankind when He shed the blood of animals, removing their skins and covered the now sin infected man and woman. God's answer to evil in the antediluvian age was to release a flood, and in doing so removing the eight out of evil. Fire fell from heaven as He delivered the "righteous Lot," and in the last days God will have the trump to sound and Jesus will meet His Bride in the clouds and therein deliver her from all evil.

Much of the teachings of the Catholic Church are not found in the scripture, and are false doctrines. False doctrine, like lies, necessitate more lies to give a foundation of plausibility. The teaching of purgatory as defined in The Catholic Encyclopedia is, "a place or condition of temporal punishment for those who, departing this life in God's grace, are, not entirely free from venial faults (sins that can be forgiven if proper penance has been made), or have not fully paid the satisfaction due to their transgressions." The teaching of purgatory is based on the Catholic teachings of sin and forgiveness.

The Catholic's teaching on sin and forgiveness can be found in the Baltimore Catechism and other church documents. The doctrine of sin as taught by the Catholic Church identifies two punishments for sin; eternal (unconfessed or unforgivable sins) and temporal, in which a person must expiate (atonement received for wrong-doing when one is attempting to undo the wrong that they have done, by suffering a penalty, by performing some penance) and make reparation (a prayer or devotion with the intent to repair the "sins of others") for his sins. Eternal sins receive eternal punishment which is exacted in hell forever.

Punishment for temporal sin is enacted in this world and in purgatory. Catholic teaching of penance and its effect on sin is explained as follows: *forgiveness of sin dispatches the eternal punishment and only part of the temporal.* The remainder of one's sin debt is paid by penance (prayer, fasting, almsgiving, works of mercy and patient suffering), remitting temporal punishment. The purpose of temporal punishment is to satisfy God's wrath that is held against the sinner for their sin, to teach the penitent the great evil of sin, and to prevent one from falling again. As found in Catechism of St. Pius X "the penitent must fully satisfy the justice of God. Satisfaction (or penance) is an act of the penitent by which he makes certain reparation to the justice of God for his sins. It must be emphasized that the primary reason for temporal punishment is to make satisfaction for sin."

MERCHANDISING SIN

The false teaching of sin and forgiveness gave birth to the false teaching of penitence, and this false teaching ushered in the false teaching of Indulgence. The false teaching of Indulgence made entrance in Catholic doctrine in 1095 when Pope Urban II forfeited all penance of persons who participated in the crusades and confessed their sins. In addition, for a sum of money, the church would forgive the penance of the ones who did not engage in the Catholic's "Holy Wars."

It was not long before this church was again fulfilling Apostle Peter's warning of false teachers when he said, "they with feigned words make merchandise of you." One of the requirements of an overseer of the Lord's Church was to not be, "greedy of filthy lucre."

The false teaching of Indulgences was not a teaching of the Lord's Church, but a teaching that grew out of the institution of the Church of Rome and its desire of "filthy lucre." The strategy of the teaching of Indulgence was to take monies from the masses of people to increase the wealth of the Catholic Church. This teaching provided for the remission of temporal punishment for sins after the sinner confesses and receives absolution (the remission of sin, or of the punishment due to sin, granted by the Church). As previously stated about these false teachings, every sin has a two-part punishment: one is eternal extracted in hell, the other is temporal and is paid in earth and after death in a dwelling place of the dead called purgatory. In the early twelfth century, the Church began claiming that it had a "treasury" of indulgences, comprising of the virtues of Jesus and the saints, which it sold to increase the wealth and power of the church.

THE TIPPING POINT

It was this flagrant violation of the very nature of the grace of God that moved Luther to rebel against the Catholic Church. Luther was a theology professor at Wittenberg University and also the priest at the City Church in Wittenberg. Luther noticed the numbers of people coming for confession had decreased significantly and the "sinners" were traveling to neighboring towns to buy Indulgences. Luther was repulsed when he saw the sale of Indulgences as a replacement of the forgiveness of sins. The teachings of the Catholic Church required the position of the priest to hear the confession of the sinner, extend absolution to the sinner, and assign proper penance. Luther also strongly believed that one lived a life of humility in order to receive God's grace. The end result of his disagreement with the church's use of Indulgences was his 95-point thesis revealing the devastating effect Indulgences had in debasing people's faith.

The use of Indulgences to create wealth for the church seemed to have no restrictions for the selling or how it was used. Indulgences grew to such wide-spread practices in the Catholic Church, it became a "privatized business opportunity," a system of sale and resale, complete with commissions. Leo X created an environment where Indulgences were sold that allowed for the reseller to keep fifty percent as profit and send the other half to Rome. There were even sales gimmicks. Albert of Brandenburg sold his Indulgences with the guarantee of complete remission of sins. His pitch? *Why face purgatory? Go straight to heaven with this Indulgence!* "But wait there's more," it seems you can almost hear Albert say when he announced his Indulgences would also allow you to propel dead loved ones into heaven and let them escape the troubles of purgatory.

Johann Tetzel, a Dominican friar who became the Grand Commissioner for indulgences in Germany, declared of the Indulgence "As soon as a coin in the coffer rings / the soul from purgatory springs." Luther addresses this levity in the twenty seventh and twenty eighth arguments against the selling of Indulgences when he writes, "They preach a man who say that as soon as the penny jingles into the money-box, the soul flies out of purgatory. It is certain that when the penny jingles into the money-box, gain and avarice can be increased, but the result of the intercession of the Church is in the power of God alone."

Martin Luther is often credited with starting the protestant movement when he nailed the Ninety-Five Thesis on the sale of Indulgences to the door of the Castle Church of Wittenberg. In reality, the Protestant movement finds its roots in John Wycliffe's attempt to reform the Roman Catholic Church, although he was largely unsuccessful. Jan Hus, a Czechoslovakian priest who was swayed by Wycliffe's theology was the main influence of Luther's uprising against the Roman Catholic's teaching of Indulgences when he wrote his 95 thesis against the use of Indulgences. It was no doubt that Martin Luther, was the "firebrand" that lit the flames of protest against the Roman Catholic Church that led to the Protestant Reformation. Luther, along with other reformers, became the first to skillfully use the power of the printing press to advance their ideas about the false teachings of the Catholic Church beyond the reach of their voice.

Luther was served notice he would be excommunicated if he did not follow the order given by the Catholic Church to renounce his Ninety-Five-point thesis. Luther responded he would not withdraw his thesis unless scripture proved him wrong. Luther conveyed to his accusers that he did not accept as truth the church's teaching of the pope being endowed as the only authority given authorization to interpret scripture. When Luther began to teach publicly his belief that scripture did not support giving the pope special understanding and ability to interpret scripture was when the Church in Rome reached a breaking point with Luther. Losing this exclusive control would overthrow and undermine the position and authority of the papacy, and the Catholic Church's power over the masses who feared eternal damnation rested in the hands of the church's presbytery.

Luther was publicly excommunicated from the Roman Catholic Church for his refusal to recant his position on the papacy and he was declared a "convicted heretic." Luther, having received a sentence of death for his heresy, lived as a fugitive from the church and while he was living in seclusion, translated the New Testament into German. The New Testament, now in the hands of the laypeople, removed the power formally held the priesthood to know and read God's words, and placed it back to the individuals that it had been seized from by the creation of the Catholic priesthood.

It was during this time of seclusion, Luther's influence grew through his prolific use of the printing press. Along with printing his bible in German, Luther distributed many publications about his views on Catholic doctrine. It is said Luther printed more literature than the combined total of all the other reformers in this period. Out of Luther's efforts to reform the Catholic Church, a movement was formed known as "Lutheranism." This movement would grow and the Lutheran Church would be born. Luther's "revolt" against the power of the church would leave a dark spot in church history. His rejection of the Catholic Church's power led for the call to emancipate the peasants of Germany. Arising out of this movement was a group called the "Evangelical Brotherhood." These men swore to liberate the peasants of Germany. Luther was frightened by this movement; his fear, along with his dependence on wealth of the princes to continue his work, caused him to renounce the revolt of peasants in violent terms, and support the princes in their suppression of the uprising. The peasants attempt to overthrow the powerful lords of the church and the abuses they were suffering came with a high price. Over one hundred thousand lost their lives, and the treatment of the surviving peasants suffered even more abusive treatment of the princes of the Lutheran Church. The suppression of the peasant revolt would be the gateway for Germany to adopt a new state religion, the Lutheran Church.

The reformation movement instigated by Luther along with John Calvin, Huldrych Zwingli, and many more reformers would create a division in the western hemisphere Christian practices. The "power of the press" was born out as a truth during this time. As much as any one man played a part in the reformation movement, it was the invention of Gutenberg's printing press that gave the ability to rapidly produce and place in the hands of masses of people the charges the reformers were making against the Catholic Church.

THE ORDER OF JESUITS

It took a while for the Roman Catholic Church to respond, but they did. At the Council of Trent, the Protestant movement was defined as heretical, and a counter reformation was launched by the Catholic Church. A new found military order was created named Jesuits and installed Ignatius de Loyola, a Spanish soldier turned priest, as its leader. The Catholic Church now refers to the Jesuits order as a missionary and education order, but they were more mercenaries than missionaries, and their schooling was administered with spears and swords. The protestant reformation and the Catholic Counter Reformation lead by the Jesuits began a religious war that left Europe in shambles. The Catholics' attempt to subjugate the groups that broke away from the Church led to entire church groups being annihilated. Over a period of time this conflict involved the major powers in Europe, and the "Thirty Year War" that followed shattered entire regions with famine and disease. It is thought that forty percent of Europe's population was lost as a result of this conflict.

The attempt to remain as the only universal church came at a high cost. Millions upon millions of lives were lost in the "Thirty Year War." Rome's strangle hold on God's word and Church was broken, and national religions were adopted. God's word was now unchained from the strangle hold of the papacy and was now becoming available to the "whosoevers" to read, study and reveal the Creator and His Son. This was a time of renewal for the Lord's Church. Around the world, liberated and unconstrained Christian Churches came from the shadows into the light, and the life and soul saving changes came from the unfettered teaching of God's word. The teaching of God's word now was advancing in the lives of people instead of the godless overlords of the Catholic Church.

Denominationalism

Matthew 16:26
For what is a man profited, if he shall gain the whole world, and lose his own soul? or what shall a man give in exchange for his soul?

Jesus' promise to Apostle Peter came to life in the history of the rule of Rome over Christendom; indeed, the gates of hell were opened against His church, but she was not destroyed. God had preserved His church, around the globe. Groups of true followers of Jesus assembled in homes and clandestine locations where the teachings of the Apostles were honored and promoted. The institution that developed around the Roman Catholic Church did not advance the Lord's church, but rather it harmed the true church. History bares out the acts of this church as evil and godless, but the Roman Catholic Church was and is still identified by many as the church of our Lord.

Hundreds of church groups were started with the declining power of the Roman Church. Most of these groups fell in one or two major divisions: *Arminianism* and *Calvinism*, and institutions grew around these new groups, often taking some of the teaching from the Catholic Church. The Arminan system of belief is associated with Jacobus Arminius, a sixteenth century theologian. The core of their teaching is the rejection of predestination and affirming the freedom of the human will; God assists in salvation but man chooses or rejects God. The Calvin system of belief originated from the theologian John Calvin in the sixteenth century. Calvinism is based around the absolute power and supremacy of God.

The "Age of Enlightenment" beginning in the Seventeenth Century allowed for a leap in knowledge and understanding of humanity. Out of this movement came "higher critical" thinking. Theologians began to look outside of the institutions they were associated with, and looked to scripture as compared to doctrinal teachings of their church discipline and other writings. This allowed them to arrive at a greater understanding of God, and mankind's relationship with Him. The result of this movement was the birth of hundreds of churches and dominations, each taking with them part of the teachings of the originating church, and adding a different view of scripture to their teachings. Just a century before, there was the Catholic Church in one group, and declared heretics in the other. The eighteenth century spawned thousands of church groups; some would endure and become major denominations lasting for centuries.

REFORMATION OR RESTRUCTURING?

With the end of the universal control over Christendom by the

Church in Rome, church groups were forming and much of the institutional structure of the Catholic Church was adopted by the "protest" churches. This movement when all things are taken into consideration, was more like a government forced corporate split when the corporation is deemed to hold a monopoly. This was more of a decentralization of power than a true reformation.

When the protest churches established the institutional framework for their denominations, it was essentially the same episcopal polity found in the Catholic Church. The top down authority polity was used to control the approved doctrines and dispense church discipline. Doubtless, these institutions were more diverse, but in the same way the Catholic Church used its structure to enforce the teachings (many of which were not scriptural), these break-away church groups modeled the same polity.

The word denomination in its simplest form means, "to give a name to." Denominations "rebrands" the Church of the Lord with an institutional name that gives a co-joined purpose. When the Lord's Church is branded with a denominational name, it will identify the true church with a doctrinal identity, and often starts with or ends with the altar-ego taking preeminence over the Lord's Church that it is co-joined with. This is not to say that all denominations are evil, but rather thy give evidence to the existence of the institution that develops around the Lord's Church.

History proves the institution that develops around the Lord's Church holds the capacity to refocus the energy and purpose of the Lord's Church, and move her away from the word of God. The result makes it difficult for the Lord's Church to exist and flourish inside this institution. The nature of an institution is to grow. The institutions that govern nations, education, hospitals and churches all will take on a life of their own, and often leave behind not only the founders but the reason they were founded. The very nature of the institution that develops around the Church is parasitical.

As a parasite grows, it often makes the host look alive and healthy but in reality it is killing the host. Mistletoe is a parasite that gives the appearance of health on the trees that hosts its growth but in reality the tree is sick and dying as the parasite draws the limited resources from the tree. As the scope of the institution broadens, it will extract the resources of time and money to support the developing alter-ego.

These resources are taken from supporting the work and purpose of the church, and soon the institution becomes the focus of the consumption of the resources. The growing institution must diversify to continue growing. Diversification in church growth can take one or two avenues to continue its growth, and often both occur as the demand for more resources arise.

AN IDENTITY CRISIS

One indication a church is being overtaken by the institution is *inclusive theology*. Inclusive theology will create an environment where the institution invites and encourages diluted theology to gain resources and people to support and continue its growth. If left unchecked the Lord's Church will lose its identity and strength to the institution.

Secondly, relevant theology will be taught. Relevant theology is when the institution engages the current culture for the practices and promotion of the institution. Growth of the institution demands a continued increase of resources and people for non-stop growth. Institutions tolerant of or adopting the community's understandings on moral and social issues comes with the suppression of God's Word. In the end, the institution and her church will be in conflict. The institution will demonize the Lord's Church as extremists who are withholding God's love and the Lord's Church will migrate out of the institutions who have changed the mission and purpose for which they were established.

The changing of the mission and purpose of the Lord's Church will build the institution, but its growth has the intended or unintended consequence of driving the Lord's Church from the institution that was built to support her.

The old adage adopted from Lord Acton "power corrupts, and absolute power corrupts absolutely," was born out as truth with the power of the Roman Catholic Church. In their attempt to remain as the universal authority, they suppressed religion, philosophy, morals, politics, art and education. The advancement in understanding—not just in religious teachings—was suppressed to keep control of the masses. The education of the general population that had been inhibited by the Catholic Church was to be reignited when the oppressive force was stayed. Knowledge grew in all of human development.

APOSTOLIC SUCCESSION

In spite of the gates of hell being opened against the Lord's Church, she still continued to meet in homes and other places in clandestine assemblies where God's word and the Apostles' teachings continued. Many denominations claim they can trace their existence all the way back to the churches founded in the bible, but the truth is the endurance of the Lord's Church did not come with church groups "passing the torch;" in fact, quite the opposite is true.

God works in the hearts of men who have been given revelation of Him. This is how faith is built, as the scripture says, "faith cometh by hearing and hearing by the word of God." As God reveals Himself in the pages of the Bible, faith is increased and God is pleased with the believer, for "without faith it is impossible to please Him." God's Church is not established or empowered by the creeds and doctrinal distinctives held and promoted by church groups.

A revelation of God brings salvation and the indwelling of the Holy Spirit to "teach all things" concerning the purpose of the Church. When two or three Spirit indwelt people are assembled, the Lord shows up and the Church is complete. Countless churches bore no names, had no creeds, and had no noted leaders from Pentecost until now. This is how the Lord's Church defeats the gates of hell.

A century and a half of denominational quarrels often ending in violence would lead to a new group of reformers rising from the ashes of church institutions. With only a few exceptions, this new group did not advance the Lord's Church but rather advanced their own denominational power.

As the protest churches were breaking out of the Catholic Church and denominations were forming over differences in doctrinal views, persecution still was exercised against groups of non-conforming believers who still gathered in secret church meetings to worship their Lord. The desire to worship God free of forced denominational decrees led many of the "secret" churches to settle in the British-held colonies of America.

THE NEW WORLD

The arrival of the church in America would change the nature and polity of the institution of the church. In the sixteenth and seventeenth centuries, many of the newly formed denominations began to populate the recently settled colonies. Anglicanism (a member of the Church of England or of a church in communion with it) and Congregationalism (developed out of the English Puritan movement) were the prevailing denominations in the majority of the colonies.

American colonies generally were filled with people fleeing from religious persecution. Protestants and Catholics alike believed a single church institution was necessary to establish uniformity of religion must exist in any given social order. This opinion was based on the belief that there was one true religion and the relationship with civil authorities should be as close as possible to impose the authority of the church, forcibly if necessary. Non-conformists could expect no mercy and might be executed as heretics.

The Church of England was established when King Henry VIII was refused church recognition for his marriage to Catherine of Aragon. The Church of England supplanted the Catholic Church and replaced the Pope's authority with the King's, and renamed it as the Church of England. The newly named church kept, with little change, the same polity and doctrines. The institutions of Anglicanism look very similar to the Catholic Church and were ready to persecute any opposing church views. Congregationalism was a part of the Non-conformists against the Church of England and were called first independents. They embraced personal responsibility of each congregation to be self-determining without any outside institutional oversight. Each church group was considered autonomous and independent. Congregationalists were not just a decentralized church group like most of the protest denominations. They rejected state and church relationships, did not place any trust in state-established religions, and supported freedom in political and religious matters.

As the populations of the colonies grew, the numbers of different church groups would grow from the "independent" ideology with the polity based on the autonomy, independency, self-determination of the church's institution, and the priesthood of the believer for the church member. In returning to the structure of the church institution as described by the Apostles, the Churches of America would be used by God to restructure His Church to be a powerful voice of God's grace and mercy that removes His wrath off of the sin-stained souls of His creation. The outcome of this expanding growth in church teaching would be a series of "awakenings" that would refocus believers to focus on God's word more than man's writings and doctrinal imperatives.

The Awakening

9

Mark 12:17
...Render to Caesar the things that are Caesar's,
and to God the things that are God's...

Evangelicalism provides a conundrum for the church historian. Evangelicals are Christians who believe a "born again" experience predicates salvation. They believe the Bible is without error, is God's revelation to humanity, and takes the great commission as a personal assignment from God to bring the Gospel message to the lost. The church historian will date the emergence of Evangelicalism in the seventeenth century, and credits the Christian Awakenings to this newly developed theology of a commitment to the Gospel message and evangelism.

The fundamental premise of Evangelicalism is the conversion of individuals from a sentence of death to a "new birth" through faith placed in the preaching of the Gospel message. The Evangelical movement gave birth to a new theological word: *soteriology*. Soteriology is constructed from two Greek terms, *soter* (Saviour or deliverer), and *logos* (word, matter or thing). Soteriology is the biblical method for forgiveness of sin and the removal of God's wrath and to the end a restoration of the sinner to God.

The doctrine of salvation had been corrupted by the false and heretic teachings of the Catholic Church and many of these teachings were carried forward in the protest movement as well as in the subsequent denominational movement. For the most part, their teachings on mankind's salvation focused on a "ransom" theology that taught Jesus' death was only a ransom payed to Satan for the lost souls imprisoned in hell, for the sin debt of the inherited sin of Adam (often referenced as *original sin*). The application of ransom theology led to methods and means, held by men in the priesthood, to release the payment for personal sin. The establishing of false teachings to relieve a sinner from a personal sin debt empowered the institutions with the authority to discharge the eternal punishment for sins committed by the sinner.

The theology behind the Evangelical Movement was not a new methodology developed for soteriology, it was a re-emergence of the teachings of the Apostles which had been sequestered for centuries by the Catholic Church and the ensuing protest denominations. The freedom from denominational control and persecution in the American colonies allowed the true Church of God to come out of the shadows of secret clandestine assemblies. These un-conforming Churches re-established the public teachings and doctrines that had been taught from the Apostles to Polycarp to Irenaeus and passed from generation to generation of believers who were willing to suffer persecution and death for the true message of their Lord.

The institution built around the church was taking on a new profile. Under the oppressive institutions of the church, the previous fifteen centuries hid the message of the Gospel under the false teachings growing out of these godless institutions, and forced the true followers of Jesus to flee and hide with their message of hope. Apostle Paul gave notice of what the outcome of this would be, "But if our Gospel be hid, it is hid to them that are lost: In whom the god of this world hath blinded the minds of them which believe not, lest the light of the glorious Gospel of Christ, who is the image of God, should shine unto them. For we preach not ourselves, but Christ Jesus the Lord; and ourselves your servants for Jesus' sake."

Both the Catholic Church and the protest denominations violated this covenant true men of God made to the Saviour concerning the Gospel message. The Church's institutional leaders not only hid the Gospel message, they preached themselves as the holders and administrators of the forgiveness of God. Satan has always been willing to let men proclaim a Gospel that keeps the souls of men chained in the darkness of sin. Even though the institutions of the church grew and prospered for the previous fifteen centuries, the Lord's Church was persecuted by these institutions and they became the enemies of God's Church. It is a reminder to the Christian Church today that amassing wealth, buildings and large crowds is not evidence of the blessing of God.

THE HALF-WAY CHURCH MEMBER

The Puritan denomination, as all of the denominational groups formed from the protest movement, took with them polity and doctrinal beliefs, as well as the church's institutional involvement in civil governmental affairs. In many of the English colonies, to vote on civil matters required good standing with a Puritan Church. As the Colonies developed, many of the second and third generation citizens were not willing to embrace much of the Puritan's teachings, and did not become members of the church. The solution to allow for civil government to continue without forfeiting the church's institutional control was the acceptance the *Half-Way Covenant* in the mid seventeenth century. This was an agreement among the churches to allow for unconverted people to have membership in the institution of the church. The expectation of the preachers was that the church's institution would continue to have influence over civil government matters to whom they received tax-supported income from and the "half-way" members would be exposed to the Gospel and would lead them to a "born-again" experience that was a requirement for full membership in the Puritan Church.

The *Half-Way Covenant* allowed full civil privileges with limited church privileges to the "half-way" members. This would soon change the purpose and mission behind the church's institution and diminish the scriptural imperatives it taught. The consequences of including non-believers in the church's institution was to dilute the membership of the institution with unbelievers and distort the purpose of the Church's institution from a refuge for the believer into a political arm of the unconverted. Once again we see the institution built to support the Lord's Church overtaking the purpose of the Church with political and financial compromises to advance not the Gospel, but the security and power of the institutions.

The Great Awakening refers to the revival movement that swept the Atlantic region in 1730's and lasted for about twenty years. It could be argued Jonathan Edwards was the one who ignited the awakening of the church with his preaching focusing on the word of God, not institutional ideology. Edwards was a Congregationalist and both he and the denomination carried with them the Calvinist theology when they separated from the Puritans. He and his colonial offshoots who were addressing the failure of the institution to proclaiming the Gospel of the Lord were identified as "New Lights."

These men saw the need for reform in the church's institutions preaching of the Gospel, and they endorsed the revival of the Church. The perceived the need to change the preaching of the Gospel was awakened by the re-emerging soteriology introduced with the Evangelical insurgence. The message of the revival sermons centered on calling people to respond to the preaching of the Gospel message with a personal repentance and forgiveness of sin.

Edwards grandfather, Solomon Stoddard, led the battle for the *Half-Way Covenant* to be adopted a century before. This covenant had redefined the purpose of the church's institution, changing the definition of church membership and filling the churches with unbelievers. The outcome of this covenant was that the power of the Gospel had been silenced by the unbelieving members in the church. God chose the grandson of the man who had led the movement that watered down the Gospel and changed the purpose of the church's institution to lead the Great Awakening.

Edwards would be the one who led the awakening of the churches. This awakening would repurpose the church's institution to be a place where God's word would be preached with power and conviction, with the outcome of lost souls coming to the hope of the Gospel.

The Great Awakening was further advanced when George Whitfield traveled to the American Colonies. Whitfield became acquainted with Charles Wesley while attending Oxford University. Wesley was a major influence in the spiritual development in Whitfield's life. While at Oxford, Whitfield became a part of a group of men led by Charles Wesley's brother John. This group gathered for the purpose of prayer, fasting and spiritual actions, and called themselves "Methodists" because they had established a methodical way to develop their spiritual growth and understanding of God's purpose for their lives.

Whitfield joined with the Wesley brothers to learn more about God's purpose for his life and was soon to help lead this group of men. Out of this group that called themselves the "Holy Club" started what would be known as the Methodist movement. Soon after graduation from Oxford, Whitfield was ordained as a minister of the Gospel and started his preaching ministry. He did not pastor any church group, but rather preached as an interim preacher and evangelist.

Whitfield took his first journey to America in 1738, just as the Great Awakening was starting to dwindle. Whitfield brought new life to the flames of revival in New England when he joined with Jonathan Edwards in Pennsylvania, helping him to continue the Awakening started by Edwards. In New Jersey, he joined with William and Gilbert Tennent who traveled with Whitefield, acquainting him to other ministers in New York, New Jersey, Delaware and Pennsylvania helping to make Whitefield's revival preaching a success.

Not everyone was pleased with Whitfield's preaching, as many of the local Church institutions had their power striped when the Gospel was preached outside the institutions they had created. The power of God that surrounded Whitfield was rejected by his detractors, and they gave credit to "showmanship" as his power to preach the Gospel, thereby denying the Great Awakening was authored by God. When Whitfield returned to England, the Tennent brothers united the scattered, local revivals into what we now call the Great Awakening. Whitfield as well worked with Samuel Davies of Virginia. Davies was a preacher in the mold of the great preachers of this age and was early influenced by Whitfield's preaching. It is said he often read the sermons preached by Whitfield in the church assemblies and Davis would assume the pulpit of Johnathan Edwards upon his death.

Whitfield's willingness to come alongside each of these preachers was instrumental to the success in the revival meetings. Tens of thousands of people who sat under his preaching, along with untold numbers who read his sermons in the newspapers and in printed materials, helped unite the scattered local revivals into the Great Awakening.

The power of the Great Awakening was no more than the unchaining of the message of the Gospel from the institutions created by men, and returning the message to the men of God. The message that was delivered to the Apostles, who in turn invested the message given them into the lives of other men, who in like manner taught other faithful men. This was God's plan for the founding and enlargement of His Church. Paul entrusted Timothy with God's plan for His Church to endure against the "gates of hell," with this command, "And the things that thou hast heard of me among many witnesses, the same commit thou to faithful men, who shall be able to teach others also." God's intent for the preservation of the message of the Gospel was never left to the cold halls of institutions built by men, but was to be written in the hearts of men and transferred from mouth to ear to heart down through all generations that would exist until Jesus arrives for His Bride.

The Awakening of the church did not start from the institutions built around the church, but rather the revivals were rejected by the "Old Lights" (church leaders who rejected the Evangelical movement that ushered in the Great Awakening). The Old Lights rejected the personalized experience in the re-emerging of the solitarily of the "born again" experience. They suspected the revival teachings were replacing intelligential understanding of the Gospel with an emotional response. The Old Lights did not consider the personal response to the revivalist preaching of the Gospel a spiritual experience, but concluded it was just a response to the passionate preaching of the evangelists. Many denominational leaders resisted the Great Awakening, supposing it was an attack against the Calvinistic teachings held by the majority of the Church institutions. The revival preaching was most effective outside of the institutions, and when the Great Revival began to lose momentum, there was a concerted effort to bring these converts under denominational control and teachings by the "Old Lights." As the Great Awakening began to lose momentum in the late eighteenth century, the church leaders tried to normalize the converts back under the teachings of the denominational institutions.

THE SECOND GREAT AWAKENING

The nineteenth century brought about a second wave of Awakening's. The Second Great Awakening instigated a profound change in the institutions of the church. The powerful denominations rising out of the Colonial era, Anglicans, Presbyterians, Congregationalist and the Reformed all had roots that were planted in the protest movement. Much of their polity reflected the top down structure of the Catholic Church, and many brought with them the false doctrine of "Ransom Theology." The institutions took an authoritative position in the relationship between the Lord's Church and the believer's relationship to the Saviour.

The numerical strength of the Baptists and Methodists were now comparative to that of the denominations dominant in the Colonial period, and was redefining how the church's institution would support the Lord's Church. The second Awakening came coupled with Christians attempting to apply Christian teaching to bring godly resolution of social problems. Social Gospel activism was born out of the second Awakening in the 19th Century. The growing numerical strength of the Baptists and Methodists occurring during the Second Awakening would soon outnumber the protest denominations and reshape how the institution of the church would interact with the Lord's Church for more than a century. This Awakening would spawn a culture in the church institution that would embrace social crusading. This call to action often was inspired by the revival meetings, and gave cause to the church's institution to engage and support the abolition movement, temperance movement, and engage prisons and mental institutions to bring changes in their structure and operation, just to name a few.

In the Second Awakening, missionary societies were established and supported by the church's institutions and would send missionaries to the uncharted West in America, Hawaii and many other places. The missionaries did not involve themselves in the culture to transform it to reflect their culture, but came to preach the Gospel to the lost natives.

Outdoor revival meetings were the normal church institution on the American frontier during the Second Awakening. These outdoor meetings were soon to be established as "camp meetings." For the most part, camp meetings were loosely organized preaching assemblies and when announced, drew crowds from farms, ranches and settlements as far away as forty miles.

It is supposed James McGready originated the camp meetings in Logan County, Kentucky. People would travel for two or three days to attend these meetings and would camp out in wagons or tents and attend revival meetings that were held in rustic outdoor churches hastily constructed for a three or four day meeting. It is reported as many as twenty thousand people would be in attendance at some of these camp meetings. There were many who came out for the excitement or social engagement, but most came to worship, pray, sing hymns and to hear the Word of God preached. Weddings and baptisms were officiated by the revivalist during the camp meetings as well. Although there would be differences in the theology of the men preaching at these meetings, a born-again experience driven by the Evangelical resurgences of the teachings of the Apostles was the purpose these men traveled and preached at these remote camp meetings.

The lack of institutional oversite was a problem to the churchmen in the denominations. They saw the structure of the camp meeting as antagonistic to order and control that the institutions created. Operating outside the authority of the institutional control, these camp meetings, the men, and their ministries were considered counterfeit works, and the churchmen refused to accept the Awakening as a legitimate movement of God.

Camp meetings played an important part for the growth of many church groups. The Methodists, Baptists, Shakers, Disciples, and Cumberland Presbyterians all grew in numerical strength during the Second Awakening.

The focus on the preaching of the Gospel kept most doctrinal teachings out of the Camp meetings. This would affect the religious and social life of the frontier in various ways. The institutions of the church previously spent most of their energy and resources establishing and enforcing denominational doctrines and creeds. The attention shifting to the preaching of the Gospel would soon lead the Church and her institution to break down the church creeds and doctrinal imperatives that drew lines of separation between the institutions. This, along with declining numbers in the colonies' denominations, would weaken the status of denominationally-approved pastors and preachers, and would allow for the rise of "unbranded" God-called men to preach the Gospel. This new church polity found agreement with the independent spirit of the frontier settlers, who mostly lived outside of the structures to which the city dwellers were accustomed.

THE AMERICAN REVOLUTION

The American Revolution sparked not only a political restructuring based on freedom from established authorities, but redefined the view of how the institutions of church would interact with civil authorities. The change in the church's polity would be reflected in the church's relationship with civil matters. The founding fathers declared, "Congress shall make no law respecting an establishment of religion, or prohibiting the free exercise thereof." In America, the church and civil authorities would be separated for the first time since the universal church movement in the second century. This change would create a new relationship the church's institution would have with both civic and religious behavior in the nation. This new relationship was to change the purpose and ministry the church would have in the daily lives of Americans. For the first time since the mid second century, the church would be unfettered from civil authority. This newfound independence was reflected in the Second Awakening; the church was becoming independent from denominational oversite. The theological teachings of Calvinism and Arminianism took a back seat to the teaching of the Apostles. A "whosoever" preaching of the Gospel opened the door of salvation to all who would hear and believe the message of the Saviour; anyone could be saved. Poor or rich, religious or heathen, freeman or slave—all were able to receive the hope of the Gospel.

Personal study of the bible was encouraged and often promoted as superior to formal training of denominational institutions. Pastors and teachers were not necessarily endorsed, licensed or ordained by the institutions, but were men called of God. The Second Awakening tore down the wall of separation built by the church's institutions, dividing the clergy from the laity. All believers stood on level ground at the foot of the cross. The indwelling of God's Spirit relieved the perceived need for clergy to intercede in man's affairs with God. There was no need for a church polity that placed God's people in forced accountability to the clergy and teachings of dependencies on man or the institution of the church. God could and would call the simple to preach and serve Him and His church.

One of the most influential revivalists of the Second Great

Awakening was Charles Finney. Finney was a lawyer practicing in New York. He was unsure about his salvation, and set time aside to contest his spiritual condition with God. After hours of prayer and soul searching, he found peace with God and assurance of his salvation. Soon after Finney's salvation, he began to preach the Gospel. As his revelation from God was growing, his secular employment as a lawyer took a back seat in his daily activities. It is said he met with a client told him, "I have a retainer from the Lord Jesus Christ to plead his cause and cannot plead yours." Finney was sure that God was calling him to a preaching ministry. Little did he know, God would raise him up to be the leading revival preacher of the nineteenth century.

Finney was ordained by the Presbyterian Church for the ministry. He was soon contacted by the Female Missionary Society of the Western District, and started his work in upper New York. Calvinism theology controlled most of the church groups, but Finney went against the teachings of the church's institutions and urged people to be converted as he preached the "whosoever" Gospel, and called on the ones who believed to publicly accept Christ. Finney established at the conclusion of his sermon the opportunity to respond to the teachings of the Gospel with a public call for repentance and acceptance of Jesus as Saviour, a practice that is still in many of the churches with an evangelical leaning today.

THE THIRD GREAT AWAKENING

As the Second Awakening was dwindling down in 1820, a new surge of revivals began starting the third wave of Awakening. The First Awakening was awaking the church institution to the scripture. For generations, theological lines had been drawn between the denominations, primarily between Calvinism and Arminianism. The teaching emphasis was on denomination distinctive prior to the Great Awakening. The preaching by the revivalist that brought about the Great Awakening abandoned the denominational "turf" and their control over the matters of salvation, and adopted some if not all of the re-emergence of the Apostle's teachings ushered in by the Evangelical movement's teachings on soteriology. The Second Awakening took the revival meetings out of the church's institutions to the people in public gatherings, leaving behind new groups that formed churches unattached to any denominations. These revival preachers often encouraged social activism.

The Third Awakening started in the 1850's and lasted until the 1900's, and had an overture of militant social activism and emphasis on personal experiences with God, leading to a pious lifestyle. The new converts and newly revived were encouraged to engage the community at large to correct social problems. This would be a new policy adopted by many of the church's institutions.

The ministry of the Gospel was once again being suppressed by the institutions formed to support her. God's intent for the church was to be a gathering place for the followers of the Saviour—to be taught, equipped, and encouraged in God's word. God's plan for the church's preaching of the Gospel message was to reveal God's love for the world, and His wrath against sin being satisfied by the sacrifice of His son. The eschatology of post-millennialism was redefining the preaching and the practice of the institutions of the church. A simple understanding of the teaching of post-millennialism is the belief that this world over time will, with proper emphases and motivation by the church, improve and eventually be worthy of the return of Jesus to rule. Furthermore, it taught that Jesus would not return to earth until humanity exercised authority over the evils of the sinful world was the message theme of many of the revival meetings during the third Awakening.

The revivalist during the Third Awakening encouraged Christians and churches to be militant in attacking the social problems in America. The motivation for the energy of the churches and believers to be redirected to social causes was simple; the sooner the environment of sin was controlled, the sooner Jesus would come and establish His Kingdom in the churches on earth and the believer would rule with Jesus over the remaining sinful people.

The Third Awakening started a new wave of denominations as the different church groups in the second movement were collected together and agreed on doctrinal and social issues. These growing denominational groups began to enlarge their numbers, assets and prestige as the expanse of the nation into the western frontier was settling into cities and towns. Missions to the vast unchurched around the globe changed as well. Emphasis was placed on buildings, religious collages and denominational seminaries. The redefining of the church's institutions changed the message and purpose of their message from the Gospel preached to change the lost condition of the soul to the Gospel preached to change the environment that was perceived as unjust or sinful, and then to attend to the needs of the soul.

Many of the denominations of the Third Awakening transitioned and became the basis for much of Christendom today. During the Third Awakening, the Baptist churches added over

200,000 members. The Methodists as well enjoyed huge numbers added to their rolls. It is believed that well over one million "converts" were added to the membership rolls of the growing denominational groups.

The Civil War also added to the changes of institutions of the church. Many groups were divided over the issues of slavery and state government rights verse federal government rights. The outcome was often division and or separation of the church groups. The institutions of the church embraced the social cause, for or against slavery. The Gospel was pushed aside once again for social causes.

THE CHURCH AND SOCIAL ACTIVISM

The Church of God's focus is not social causes, although many times the institutions will engage social issues at the expense of the mission of the Lord's Church. The Apostle Paul confronting slavery in the New Testament church did not speak to the injustice of slavery but remind both the slave and slave owner they had a bond in Christ that superseded social conditions of their time. Paul, speaking about the runaway slave Onesimus who had become a believer of the Gospel and a brother in Christ to Onesimus' owner Philemon, reminded him, "For this perhaps is why he was parted from you for a while, that you might have him back forever, no longer as a bondservant but more than a bondservant, as a beloved brother—especially to me, but how much more to you, both in the flesh and in the Lord."

The emotional and experiential environment coupled with the activism presented by revival preachers of the Third Awakening created the platform for a new movement of this waking. The

Holiness Movement would change the character and practice of many of the church's institutions. The holiness movement has its roots in the Methodist denomination, dating to the mid 1800's. This movement was one defined by a lack of biblical teaching and a focus on personal experience, and had strong Arminian overtones to its teaching. The stated goal of the Holiness Movement was to embrace sanctification and transformation by conquering sins as enumerated by the revivalist preachers, to achieve power over the desires of sin, and not simply to embrace a conversion experience that brought about salvation.

Pentecostalism was born out of the Holiness Movement, and the later Welsh Revival would introduce into Christendom a new twist in practice and ministry of the church. The Pentecostals added to the Holiness teaching an experience they called a "baptism in the spirit" or "baptism of the Holy Ghost." The evidence of "speaking in tongues," demonstrated as an ecstatic utterance of untellable words, along with the re-emergence of the practice of the gifts of the Apostles. The salvation experience was not what enabled this gift, but this gift was what enabled salvation to be engaged in the life of a believer. This movement was facilitated primarily by women, and was emotionally driven. Many preachers abandoned the scripture and depended on "Words of Knowledge" or current, specific revelation from God directly to the preacher.

Many of the noted Theologians rejected the "Welsh Revival" worship practices as dangerous to the soul and spirit of the convert. G.H. Pember wrote extensively of his opposition to this type of worship espoused by the Welsh Revival. Pember and other theologians rejected many of the teachings as unscriptural, causing God's word to be devalued by the current revelation preaching. This preaching also promoted women in the preaching and pastoral ministry. The Welsh Revival was embracing and opening the door for false teachings to abound with the amending of the scripture with the "word of knowledge" as practiced by the leaders of this movement.

The Holiness Movement was not well received in the Methodist church leadership, and the results was the forming of several new Holiness denominations. The Church of the Nazarene, the Church of God, Christian Science, and the Salvation Army all have roots in the Holiness Movement. After a few years, the Assembly of God would be birthed and shortly after, the Charismatic movement would make its presence known in church's institutions.

In less than two hundred years, the Awakening of the Church from the time of Jonathan Edwards until the Welsh Revival would affect more changes on the church and her institutions than the previous fifteen centuries of church history. Most of the modern day non-Catholic church institutions can, to one degree or another, trace their church history to and through the revival preaching that the Awakenings brought to pass.

Although the founding fathers of America were influenced by Christianity, and reflections of at least Deism can be seen in the founding documents of America, the true identity as a Christian nation was forged in the "revival preaching" and the following "camp meetings" of the Awakenings. In less than a century after establishing a national identity as a nation ruled by Christian ideology driven by the institutions of the church, we will witness America's status as a Christian nation diminish into the "Post-Christian Era."

How Technology Influenced the Institutions of the Church

CHAPTER

10

Matthew 24:14
*And this gospel of the kingdom shall be preached
in all the world for a witness unto all nations;
and then shall the end come.*

I f Gutenberg's press was the power behind the reformation of Martin Luther's protest against the Catholic Church, the circuit riding preachers and the Camp Meetings were the driving force of the Awakenings, and technology will define the Twentieth Century church institution.

As the preaching moved out of the institutions of the church during the different phases of the Awakenings, denominationally distinctive teachings took a back seat to the proclaiming of the Gospel. It was not unusual to have preachers from different denominational backgrounds working together to preach the Gospel as the westward expansion spread out to the American population.

These revivalists were reaching out to settlers in the expansion and to the groups of pioneers who had settled before the expansion of the west was underway. Along with the revivalist preachers from the mainline denominations, preachers who were self-taught and un-attached to any denomination were advancing the move away from the institutional denominational control. D.L. Moody was an example of how the development of the Nineteenth Century church institution was influenced by men who would not have denominational approval.

Moody had only a fourth grade education and did not pursue any recognized theological training. He was influenced by the works of Charles Spurgeon, but for the most part he was not a reader of other men's writings. Moody's learning style was conversational; he would engage preachers with biblical questions and ask their opinions about current events of the day. Moody, in his travels to Ireland, met Henry Moorhouse, one of the prominent evangelists in the mid nineteenth century in England.

While in Ireland, Moody invited Moorhouse to Chicago, and this visit would refine Moody's preaching and ministry. Moorhouse preached the bible and not denominational distinctives. He told Moody if he would stop preaching his words and preach God's words, God would use him to do good. Moody purposed from that point forward to preach only God's word. Moorhouse died a few years later at the age of forty leaving behind the legacy of, "the man who moved the man who moved millions." In the book, "The Life of D.L. Moody" written by his son, a chapter is devoted to the impact of Henry Moorhouse on Moody's life and work. In his book, Moody's son would record, "Moorhouse taught Moody to draw his sword full length, to fling the scabbard away and enter the battle with a naked blade." Moody's time with Moorhouse would change his preaching content and style; from this point forward, he would preach only from the Bible.

It is recorded that one of Moody's detractors said, "I want you to know I do not believe in your theology." "My theology!" Moody exclaimed. "I didn't know that I had any. I wish you would tell me what my theology is." Moody was not claiming his ignorance but he was making a statement about his ideology. Moody was a bible teacher—a layman who refused to be ordained and would not be called Reverend. He preferred to be called Mr. Moody, and would not engage in or be engaged in the denominational apologetics that preoccupied the institutional churches' leadership. Moody's rejection of denomination "branding" achieved by religious education in denominationally approved educational institutions would establish the platform for the next century's church leaders.

"SUNDAY" SERVICES

Billy Sunday would be the preacher who would bridge the nineteenth century church to the twentieth century. Sunday was cut from the same fabric as Moody. Unlike Moody, Sunday was a reader and self-taught in his personal "seminary" held in his library. His personal library contained over six hundred well used books, noted with his handwriting. Sunday was ordained by the Presbyterian Church, but for all intents and purposes, he was not aligned with the denomination in any way, including their Calvinist theology. Sunday did not attend seminary and was open in his aspiration *not* to be a theologian or a part of the denominational intellectual class.

Like D. L. Moody, Sunday was born into poverty and had little formal education. Sunday was athletic and played major league baseball. He was exposed to the Gospel through the street ministry of the *Pacific Garden Mission*, and in a short time gave his life to Christ. He would soon leave his profession of baseball and enter the ministry. In less than five years after his conversion, he would become the assistant of Wilbur Chapman who was one of the most popular and well known evangelists in America. Chapmen was well educated, dressed the part, and preached with a sophisticated message, delivered with a dignified style. As Chapman's front-man, generally taking care of necessary details for the meetings, Sunday often preached and developed his preaching style that did not reflect Chapman's sophisticated and dignified manner.

Chapman mentored Sunday, helping him in his sermon construct and presentation. Sunday sat under Chapman's preaching and studied his style and structure. Additionally, Chapman inspired Sunday's desire for biblical knowledge and growth by stressing the importance of prayer. When Chapman returned to the pastorate, Sunday assumed control over the evangelic revival meetings. Where Chapman was refined and dignified, Sunday's preaching was often crude and unconventional. His vocabulary was course and rough, reflecting language habits developed after years in professional sports. He was often the target of the denominational churchmen and was publicly criticized for his crude style. Sunday would not be side tracked by his detractors, but simply responded with, "I want to preach the Gospel so plainly that men can come from the factories and not have to bring a dictionary."

Sunday would become the nation's best known evangelist

with his ability to reach both the working and professional class people with the Gospel. By the early twentieth century, he would have some of the largest crowds of any evangelist of or before his time. It is thought Sunday preached to more than one hundred million people in over twenty thousand revival meetings during his ministry. Nearly half a million people attended in a six-week period in 1923 alone.

This six-week period would prove to be the climax of Sunday's ministry. The number and size of the meetings would decline rapidly, along with his influence in the Christian circles. Many suggestions have been made about his rapid decline. Sunday credits Satan's attacks as the source of the decline of his ministry. Some credit his decline in prominence to his wealth and rise in popularity among the wealthy and political class. Others claim his decline was because of his unwillingness to take direction from his staff and modernize his ministry.

There may be one more reason for the decline of attendance Billy Sunday experienced in his revivals. Mass communications would change the way the revivalist would reach the masses of people, and this fact may have been overlooked by church historians reviewing the life and times of Billy Sunday. On January 2, 1921, the same year Sunday's rapid decline in revival attendance was beginning, a radio station in Pittsburgh aired the first religious service in the history of radio from Pittsburgh's Calvary Episcopal Church.

Religious radio broadcasting that begin in 1921 would redefine how revivalist preachers would reach the crowds. In the mid 1930's, over fifty percent of all homes in America would have a broadcast radio, and over fifty million people at any given time were available to be influenced by the radio broadcasts. A new method of evangelism was developing; no longer would mass evangelism take place in brush arbors, camp meetings, or circus tents. A man and a microphone connected to the radio could speak to more people in one broadcast than Sunday reached in his greatest six-week period when he preached to almost a half a million people. The power of mass communications through the invention and rapid assimilation of radios in the homes of America would create a new institution of the church, and would have a profound impact on the Lord's Church.

In 1923, church owned broadcast licenses for churches rated number seven out of the top 20 businesses that held broadcasting licenses. The institution of the church for centuries had been established in a geographic location and an expressed time for the assembly of the church to take place. It was at this location, people came often under distress to pay homage to God and the men who assumed priestly duties over them.

In the Awakenings, a paradigm shift in the position the institution of the church would have in the lives of people was birthed. Not only was the importance of the clergy being undermined by the teaching of salvation resting completely between God and the convert, but the teaching of the "priesthood of the believer" removed the power many of the church's institutions held over people's spiritual lives and eternal hopes.

In the centuries before the Great Awakening, people would travel to the appointed place at the appointed time to experience God. The Awakening changed that paradigm and it was replaced with the "minister" coming to the people. The revivalist who was to aspire to the call of the Gospel by the evangelical movement traveled to where the "lost souls" were gathered and brought "church" to them. The American view of the institution of the church was shifting from a place people came to give sacrifices of money and possessions, and to experience the ministry of the clergy, to a place they would hear God's word and be motivated to take action on what they had learned in their homes and communities.

TECHNOLOGY AND SOCIAL ACTIVISM

At first, many church groups and preachers rejected the concept of the radio as a part of the ministry to be endorsed by the church. Some even gave credit to Satan for the evil of radio, and others would resist using the radio for broadcasting the Gospel. Over time, most of the churches of America embraced the radio. Churches applying for broadcast licenses grew so rapidly, the government had to place limits on the numbers of religious broadcast licenses.

Radio broadcasting would ignite a new fire of social activism that had its roots in the Awakenings when the revivalist attached social change as a part of the effects of the Gospel. Preachers would launch political campaigns opposing behaviors and demanding their Christian world view to be imposed on unbelievers. Their ideology was to prepare the way for the Amillennial view of the return of the Lord to rule on earth as it was improved due to the social impact of the church.

The churches' intent to use the radio to extend the reach of a church's institutional ministry would soon be supplanted. Radio would not become so much of an extension of the church but would become separated from the institution of the church as a para-church organization. This new institution of radio grew its own congregations with an institutional church-type experience, and often competed with the church for financial resources. To many of the listeners, the radio services would become a new church institution they would claim as their church identity. They could have a church-like experience without ever leaving their homes. The first "radio church" made its appearance April 1923 under the ministry of R. R. Brown, who called his radio listeners a World Radio Congregation, and many soon would follow in R. R. Brown's footsteps.

The Twentieth Century Church in America

II Corinthians 6:14

*Be ye not unequally yoked together with unbelievers:
for what fellowship hath righteousness with
unrighteousness? and what communion hath light
with darkness?*

The twentieth century church institutions grew in power and wealth as converts were solicited for membership and funds to expand the church's influence in social matters. The marriage of social activism with the institution of the church as preached by the revivalist of the Third Awakening would create an environment of social engendering by the church's institutions. Much of the time the church groups found favor with the political class because members could be motivated to vote in mass for a political candidate or political party. As the church institutions continued to grow in prosperity and power, the political influence they gained allowed the church groups to engage in social change more than ever before experienced outside of a formal arrangement of the church and civil authority.

The institutions of church often put aside denominational differences and flexed their collective influence to sway lawmakers to implement laws that reflected the social changes espoused by the institutions. With this new found purpose in the institutions of the church, and a desire to impose their Christian world view on America's population, Christian and non-Christian alike joined with the emerging technology of mass communications of radio, television, and by the end of the Twentieth Century the World Wide Web, and would forever change the Lord's Church in America and the institutions that grew around her. This new view of the purpose of the church in America (becoming an active force of change in the social affairs of the nation) would change not only the way the message of the Church would be preached, but would morph its message from the proclaiming of the Gospel message of redemption and forgiveness by a Holy God to a message of redemption, forgiveness and a Christian activism.

The goal of changing the American social environment to reflect to the world view of the leaders of the evangelical movement was carried forward from the Third Awakening and the theology that drove much of the revival preaching in the previous three decades. The Amillennial theology of the revivalist drove much of the social activism of the institutions of church as they would pave the way for the return and rule of Jesus on earth.

MASS COMMUNICATIONS

The advent of mass communications allowed the church's institutions to take their message to church members of different denominations and church groups seeking to advance their ideology, and thereby grow in numerical and financial strength. On any given day, the mass-media preachers would claim messages that would often conflict with one another, each claiming to know the true way to gain God's favor. Skepticism of the conflicting messages caused many to reject formal institutional Church relationships and form their own theology that would allow for the advancement of an inter-denominational or non-denominational brand of Christianity.

Radio and television preachers would soon create large Christian institutions that had little or no affiliation with the traditional church institutions, and would amass great wealth and political power in the Twentieth Century. This inter-denominational movement also opened the door and gave a platform for ministries such as faith healers and false teachers of prosperity that played on the emotions and physical needs of the listeners.

A sound argument can be made that the co-joining of the church institutions and mass-media ushered in what many call a Fourth Awakening that took place in the middle of the Twentieth Century.

The Fourth Great Awakening followed in the wake of World War II as the nation was returning from a war time economy and national healing from the war itself.

The effect of mass-media allowed for the message of conservative denominations to have a larger platform than ever before and the result was the "mainstream" Protestant Churches rapidly declined in numerical and political influence as denominations like the Southern Baptist grew exponentially. The rise of the influence of the politically conservative church groups had an impact on many of the mainstream Protestant Church institutions.

Many leaders in these institutions responded to the conservative social agenda by rejecting the traditional approach to scripture and moral imperatives delineated in the Bible and had in-house theological skirmishes that led to a decline in membership as well as in political power.

BILLY GRAHAM INFLUENCE AND THE INTER-DENOMINATIONAL MOVEMENT

It was during the Fourth Awakening that Billy Graham Ministries would gain worldwide attention. Graham was a product of the inter-denominational movement of the Twentieth Century. He was rejected by a local youth group because he was too "worldly" and after attending a series of revival meetings preached by Mordecai Ham Jr, an Independent Baptist evangelist and a noted temperance movement leader, converted to Christianity at age 16.

Graham attended Bob Jones University and left after one semester stating his contempt for the legalism of the University. Graham's crusade ministry began soon after the end of World War II, in 1947 at the age of twenty-nine. Graham held his first public meeting September of 1947 and was attended by six thousand people and he would hold more than four hundred crusades on six continents during his ministry.

Graham crossed all denominational lines including the Catholic Church in building his Crusade ministry. Graham said he, "had the privilege of seeing the Pope on several occasions at the Vatican." When asked about the death of Pope John Paul II Graham replied, "I almost feel as though one of my family members has gone. I loved him very much..." Graham considered Pope John

Paul II as his "brother" and an evangelist. When Graham was asked about the spiritual condition of the Pope allowing him into heaven he responded, "There may be a question about my own...I think he's with the Lord, because he believed. He believed in the Cross...He was a strong believer."

The union Graham established between the evangelical movement and the Catholic Church would expand the reach and power of his ministry like no one ever before. Besides blurring the lines of separation between the oppressive institutions of Rome found in centuries of church history, Graham's acceptance of Catholics as brothers would cause many to redefine the soteriology established by the teachings of the Apostles. The intended or unintended effect of Graham's acceptance of the Catholic Church as "brothers" would cross all denominational lines and would re-define the history of the church.

Modeled after D.L. Moody's "sawdust trail," Graham extended an invitation to the attenders of his Crusade to respond to the messages he preached. Graham's front team would spend up to a year preparing the local church groups to take part in the crusades and to work among the ones who would respond to his invitation to come forward and receive Christ. Millions of people attended Graham's Crusades and the converts were to be funneled back into the local church groups. The Graham Crusade's use of radio and television would redefine how the institutions of the church would approach the spreading of their messages. Tens of thousands would attend his Crusades but millions would see or hear the Crusades when broadcast and re-broadcast on radio and television.

As Graham targeted his message to the "lost," a new approach to broadcast religion would be launched. The objective of these religious programs was not to preach the Gospel to the lost, they sought to attract the masses of Americans who were disenfranchised and were looking for anyone or anything to help them overcome their failures and the inequities of their lives.

Many Christian radio and television programs would soon be established and compete with the church's institutions for devoted followers, money and power. For the most part, these programs sought to attract people with a message of prosperity, health and spiritual power. The message of the Bible was marginalized with the intended purpose of attracting as many followers as possible, and financial empires were built from the offerings received from the millions of potential contributors.

There was a new emphasis on a personal relationship with Jesus during The Fourth Awakening, a message that would disregard the importance of the local assembly of believers. Out of this "Jesus movement" there would be an explosion of growth in "non-denominational" churches that espoused little or no doctrinal distinctives. The focus of these new church groups would be people-centric rather than God-centric. They often refused to be branded "churches" instead they took on names that did not identify them with the Christian church. The rise in the non-traditional approach of Christianity gave birth to the megachurches, many who preached a doctrine free message that would be attractive to the masses.

A Neo-Pentecostal movement would gain traction during this Awakening. In the sixties there would be a shift from the preaching the Gospel to preaching the "gifts" including faith healing, ecstatic utterances and current revelation. The Charismatic movement was born out of this Neo-Pentecostal movement.

The Charismatic movement invoked an emotional response to

a message focused on the establishment of a spiritual life through exercise of the spiritual gifts. The Charismatic movement was not a denominational or even an inter-denominational movement. People who identified with the Charismatic movement would often remain in their local church groups while attending, supporting, and identifying with the Charismatic movement, which would commonly debase the teachings and doctrines held by the church groups they attended. This movement would also cross the forbidden line of separation that Protestant and Catholics had mutually accepted as un-crossable before Graham's ministry.

The change in the Christian institutions during this Awakening would bring about a transformation in how America's population would respond to the influence of the churches. The secular movement was gaining traction in the sixties and seventies, and the rejection of Christian values and morals would be the fuel that drove America to the post-Christian era. For over a century, the church institutions had led a secular battle to outlaw behavior that was not in agreement with the church's institutions. Christian activists would influence lawmakers, and laws were crafted to make civil law enforce punishment of behavior they found as unacceptable. These laws were to be binding on Christians and non-Christians alike. The secular movement was joined with the progressive groups in the political and church institutions to create a base of power that would contest the power and message of the church's social agenda.

How America Arrived in the Post-Christian-Era

CHAPTER
12

II Timothy 4:2
Preach the word; be instant in season, out of season;
reprove, rebuke, exhort with all longsuffering and doctrine.

Amerida was considered a Christian nation only in as much as her citizens invoked and practiced Christian ideology. Today, like many nations that had once been considered Christian nations and have fallen into secularism, America has reached a breaking point where secularism has overtaken the Christian foundations of civil and public ideology. The number of Americans self-identifying as "Christian" has steadily decreased over the past several decades. The number of people who reject any religious identification has grown to second in number, only to the people who self-identify as evangelicals. Seven out of ten people in America still identify as Christians, but over the past several decades, attendance in religious institutions on a weekly basis has steadily declined.

When Americans are asked if they attended a religious service on a weekly basis, forty percent responded yes but when you check the religious institution's attendance records, less than seventeen percent of the population attends religious services on any given week.

With the declining attendance in the religious institutions came a loss of teaching on moral absolutes. The youth in the sixties began to challenge the authority of all institutions that exercised control over what was acceptable, moral behavior, including religious institutions. Society's attitude regarding what was considered acceptable and unacceptable behavior in the culture of America's communities began to change to reflect the acceptance of behaviors and laws that would redefine and normalize what once was forbidden or considered taboo in most of the communities in America.

As America became more secular, the nation elected political office holders that were not beholding to the religious institutions and were more influenced by the secular groups who put their money behind their political campaigns. As a result, they appointed Federal Judges who would reflect the secular ideology that put them in office. The judges soon began to challenge state laws and find unconstitutional the laws they found objectionable because they had religious overtones.

Biblical teachings were soon considered in violation of the first amendment. Educators in public schools were soon forbidden to read or even refer to biblical principles in classroom settings. Religious symbols on public property were found in violation of these same Judges. The ACLU (American Civil Liberties Union) took it upon themselves to rid America of any religious overtones except in the homes and institutions they were founded upon.

To be successful in America once required a person to promote and live by biblical laws, principles, and customs. This is not to imply that the darkness of sin and moral decay did not exist in the previous history of America. Such behavior was not considered acceptable and often times was considered illegal in the laws and social customs that were constructed to reflect natural and biblical law.

Sin and sinful behavior was shunned and often pushed into the dark corners of society. Babies were still born out of wedlock, but instead of sending out shower invitations to celebrate the birth of an illegitimate child, often the young mother was sent away to give birth as families tried to keep from shame from both the family and faith community. Homosexual behavior was still practiced at the three percent that exists today, but this behavior was declared a mental illness by the medical community and was treated as such in American culture and society.

A social progressive movement would soon take over most of the institutions of higher learning and would produce civil leaders, educators and leaders of the church's institutions that would become the driving force of social change in America. The social progressives understood that to change America's culture, it would be necessary have the institutions that had framed the culture they were altering to be a part of the change. Many religious communities were a part and are still a part of the movement to abandon natural and biblical law, and to bring America into a secular society.

As large mainstream denominations began losing membership and thereby influence in the fabric of our society, they struggled on how to recover from their downward spiral. These institutions found themselves in a situation not unlike the Puritan churches struggling to remain relevant in the newly formed colonies and became easy targets for the people bent on social change. The Puritan Churches adopted the half-way theology allowing membership without a "born again" experience and the struggling institutions adopted a "community" approach to membership, allowing for not just attendance but participation in programs and teaching positions in the groups. The unbelieving attenders in these church institutions would become the next generation's church leaders and like the Puritans would lead to a church without Christian leadership.

These church groups' institutions would soon be taken over by undegenerated leadership. Social progressives invaded these church groups and began to promote social justice for all people, regardless of their moral standing with God's Word. The theological tricks they used to press these changes were: God views all sin the same, humans are forbidden to place moral standards on others because they are not perfect, and most importantly the Bible is not the word of God, but rather it is a collection of writings that may contain the suggestions of God. Their false arguments are filled with misused, misapplied, and outright perversions of what the Bible records. They often frame their ideology with, "you cannot legislate morality." It is true you cannot legislate morality, but you can legislate what will be acceptable and unacceptable behavior in a society. In the 1960's, lawmakers and political groups in America chose to throw off any religious ideology and embrace a path that would make America a secular society.

As Americans became more secular and less religious in their beliefs, civil laws that were once based on Christian principles were replaced with laws that were not influenced by natural or biblical law. Law makers and political groups set out to remove biblical principles from current laws and constructed agendas to remove any religious or moral consideration as new laws were being drafted that would redefine how America would view sin and acceptable moral behavior.

America has been engaged in a cultural war for the past several decades. The social progressive movement has structured a pathway that will erase the impact of God and His Church in the creation, development, and divine protection of America. Their goal is to establish a civil government that is void of any moral absolutes. The social progressives are not trying to create a government structure that allows for individual freedom and liberty. The underlying goal is to restructure America for the purpose of the regulation of behavior, to remove the ability to challenge what is moral or immoral actions and to punish anyone who does not agree with their cultural understanding.

As a result of the efforts of the social progressives, history has been re-written to remove Christian influences, from the founding fathers and the constitution to the providence of God that makes us an exceptional as, "one nation under God." Public school history books over the past three decades have been steadily erasing the finger prints of God and His Church. In today's history books, most if not all teachings of the influence of the Lord's Churches in America's history is removed or recast as a hindrance to the rise of this great nation.

America as a nation supports the killing of babies; it is estimated 60 million children have been aborted in the United States alone since the Supreme Court's ruling of Roe vs. Wade, and many of the church's institutions remained silent or approved of a "woman's right to choose." The sexual revolution beginning in the nineteen sixties has eroded the moral fiber of America. The opening of the door of national approval of consenting adult's rights to engage in sexual activities with societal approval led to many of the church's institutions to remain silent on the sins of a sexual nature. The attack launched by the social progressives on the institution of marriage had little trouble in the legislative and judicial branches of our government in re-writing thousands of years of world history concerning homosexual marriage. Many of the churches' institutions have embraced or remained silent on this issue.

There is no question America was established without a national religion. However, it is equally true as long as the American people believed, practiced and proclaimed Christian biblical teachings America would be guided by Christian principles. It has been said that in America we have the government we deserve. America's political system allows for the citizens of America to vote and place in office the men and women who not only establish the laws of the land, but set the vision and the pathway of the future that will lead the nation on the course that will be inherited by the upcoming generation.

In America, the old axiom has been born out as true, "what parents take in moderation children will take to excess." America's greatest generation returning from World War II ushered in a financial recovery from the Great Depression as America's factories moved from a wartime economy to a peace time economy. America was to experience one of the greatest increases in prosperity in her history, but it would come with an associated cost. This generation would not just establish a self-indulgent population with the increasing prosperity, but a new understanding of the importance the church's institutions would occupy the daily lives of America's population.

THE CHURCH AND AMERICA'S PROSPERITY

The growing affluence of the American people would refocus their understanding of how their relationship with God and the institution of church would be reconstructed. The nation's view of God and church were moving from a national mindset of dependency created during the uncertainty of war, to a nation focused on creating wealth for personal advancement and desires. A nation that had called on God for His protection and power to give victory over their enemies now called on God for personal success, possessions and assets.

Trying to bring the church back into the social experience of America was advanced with new ministries. Among the development of these outreach based ministries was the development of "youth ministries," and they would hold the most profound effect on the church and her institutions in the Twenty-First Century.

In the early 1940's the first attempt to draft the youth back into the church's institutions was established by a Presbyterian pastor Jim Rayburn. Rayburn established a weekly club for the unchurched youth that was activity based. A short gospel presentation at the end of the meeting was presented in an attempt to establish to those attending that *church can be fun*. Out of this club would be the creation of *Young Life*, established as a para-church organization in 1941. This attempt of bringing the unchurched youth of America back to the church's institutions would be repeated and morphed time after time for the next several decades. The church's philosophy of bringing unchurched youth into the church to build institutional growth would be translated into adult attendance and would change not only the social landscape of the church but would change how and if the Gospel of the Apostles would be presented.

The door was cracked open by this generation, for the church's institutions became community focused, and the response of the institutions was to construct an atmosphere attractive to a civic and community experience. The 1950's found the church's institutions fading in importance in the community as people found new ways to experience community activities. As individual prosperity increased, America's industry looked to the development and growth of social activities outside of the church's institutions to capture some the growing wealth of the American people.

The automobile found a new purpose during this time. The family car became more than transportation, it became a symbol of the financial success of the American family and became the center of social activities for the youth. The family car, drive-in eating establishments, and Saturday night gatherings at schools and civic centers was soon to have a major influence on how the youth engaged their social life in America.

Church group leaders attributed the decline in the importance the church held in the daily lives of the American people to a lack of embracing the cultural changes. The church's institutions response to these cultural changes was to refocus its structure to compete with culture in their communities in order to attract people to the institutions.

Over seven decades have passed trying to normalize the Christian Church's institutions back as the center of social activity in American's lives. It is not difficult to conclude that it has been a failure; billions of dollars have been spent on ministries, paid staff, and buildings in an attempt to integrate church activities into the daily lives of the American people, *without success*.

The same mistakes made by the revivalist of the Third and Fourth Awakenings, in their attempt to affect spiritual change in America by establishing laws to regulate behavior was repeated in this attempt by the churches to remain "relative" in the changing culture of America.

The Lord's Church was never intended to be the social center of a civil population. The Lord's Church is designed to be the gathering place for the outsiders and wayfarers (as categorized by the world), created by the work of the Holy Spirit who is received when the Apostles' Gospel is preached and established in the lives of the followers of Jesus. Apostle Peter, describing the relationship held by the Lord's Church said, "But ye are a chosen generation, a royal priesthood, an holy nation, a peculiar people; that ye should shew forth the praises of Him who hath called you out of darkness into his marvelous light: Which in time past were not a people, but are now the people of God: which had not obtained mercy, but now have obtained mercy."

The attempt to broaden the nature and purpose of the church to include reaching out and drafting the unchurched into the institution was not the design of the Lord's Church. This method can only be "successful" when the teaching of morality, commitment, and exclusivity of the cross are mitigated, and teachings proclaimed from the pulpit are palatable to the current culture.

The attempt to normalize the church in the ever-changing culture of America places the churches' institutions at a crossroad of American history. With the current shift in the civil government endorsement and giving civil rights standing to moral behaviors found to be in contradiction with biblical teachings, the churches' institutions will be forced to change. If these church institutions are to remain a part of the national fabric, they will be forced to change biblical teachings on issues of morality. If they do not submit to changing their positions on biblical teachings, social pressure and civil law will end their relationship with the community they were trying to engage.

The Fourth Awakening ended in the late nineteen seventies and early eighties. The ending of this Awakening marked the beginning of the Post-Christian Era. The arrival of the nineteen eighties ushered in a new secular anti-moral and anti-religious movement. The morals and ethics established by the social engineering of the church's institutions were being challenged in the civil courts and were being overturned. Battle after battle was launched to remove the fingerprints of Christian influence from the laws of America. Soon prayer, the bible, and Christian symbols would be attacked as un-American and courts and law-makers would overturn or rewrite laws to embrace and promote a secular culture acceptable in a Post-Christian era.

For the most part, the main-stream Christian institutions were focused on rebuilding their influence in America's culture. Church attendance was in decline and their political power was fading. In the Twentieth Century, social change by Christian political influence had moved from the church's institutions into para-church organizations to lobby and influence the governmental structure in America. The Republican Party was adopted by the Christian social activist   movement to host its political agenda. Millions of dollars were raised along with millions of votes to be cast if the party espoused the ideology of the supporters of the movement.

THE MORAL AGENDA

The moral argument had shifted from the individual expressing personal convictions and biblical ideology to church institutions collectively lobbying for political change to reflect their Christian world view. When the influence of the church's institutions continued to decline, the political base relocated to para-church organizations, amassing people from across Christendom to establish a powerbase to punish or advance individuals or political parties to impose their Christian world view on America as secular laws.

The secular movement was adopted by the Democratic Party to host their political social crusade. The different political groups promoting their world view of secular morality collected together to create a powerbase to punish and reward political candidates and parties that would impose their world view on Christians and non-Christians alike.

The argument of biblical moral behavior had been ripped from the personal convictions of the converted hearts, and placed in the political arena to be contested, accepted or opposed not by biblical imperatives espoused by born-again followers of Christ. The biblical world view of the Christian that is established by changes authored by God in the life of a follower of the Saviour in issues of morality now was represented in the public by political parties that cannot change hearts or minds. The attempt to establish laws to regulate moral behavior in the political arena did not change minds, hearts, or behaviors of America—it only made immoral behavior legal.

The work of the Holy Spirit is the only avenue available to mankind that will change the world view of a person, community or nation. The preaching of the Gospel was never intended to create a political theocracy to host the Lord's Church. The biblical teaching concerning a follower of God is upon conversion to withdraw from an immoral environment and embrace the teachings and the people of God. Jesus prayed for His Church not to be of the world while in the world. When addressing the evil of the culture of Corinth, Apostle Paul gives this advice to the believers, "Wherefore come out from among them, and be ye separate, saith the Lord, and touch not the unclean thing," he encouraged the believers in Corinth to establish an identity with God's people and not to accept or be involved in the evil of their culture. Apostle Paul as well instructed the believers who were citizens of Corinth, "Be ye not unequally yoked together with unbelievers," as a response to the evil in Corinth.

As the power and influence of the church's institutions and her surrogate para-church organizations were failing, a policy of, "the enemy of my enemy is my friend" was accepted to assist in the attempt to turn back the rise of the secular movement. The welcoming in of false religions and cults increased their numbers as they waged a war against the secular movement. The decision to include these groups violated Paul's teaching of being unequally yoked together, and the intended or unintended outcome of this decision was the Christian church institutions normalized the cult and false religion doctrines. In essence, they had blurred the lines separating the Church of God from the false teachings of the cults.

CHRISTIANS AND POLITICAL CHANGE

The political structure of America is a representative democracy and Christians and non-Christians alike have been given the privilege of participating in our nation's political structure. America was not established as a Christian nation with the selection and promotion of a national religion. The founders of our nation made this clear when they established the verbiage of the first amendment in our constitution, "Congress shall make no law respecting an establishment of religion, or prohibiting the free exercise thereof." The design of our nation is to allow the "free exercise" of religion in the American experience.

It is well within the designs of our governmental structure for individuals, church groups and para-church organizations to engage and to seek changes in the laws that govern our nation. Seeking to establish a moral environment for people to live and raise their families is a noble goal for all in America to seek.

When the church's institutions and her segregates became engaged in political movements to change the behavior of America's citizens to reflect their Christian world view, this was a departure from the biblical approach to how the Lord's Church was to engage the "world." God's intent for the preaching of the Gospel is not to change behavior. Apostle Peter is clear on the outcome of this approach to the Gospel, "But it is happened unto them according to the true proverb, The dog is turned to his own vomit again; and the sow that was washed to her wallowing in the mire." When the attempt to legislate America as a Christian nation failed, the pig indeed returned to its mud and the dog to its vomit as law after law was challenged in the courts or re-written by the legislators or was not enforced by the American justice system.

Apostle Paul gave Timothy the key of success for the Lord's Church living in times when the teachings of God are rejected by the culture, "Preach the word; be instant in season, out of season; reprove, rebuke, exhort with all longsuffering and doctrine. For the time will come when they will not endure sound doctrine; but after their own lusts shall they heap to themselves teachers, having itching ears; And they shall turn away their ears from the truth, and shall be turned unto fables. But watch thou in all things, endure afflictions, do the work of an evangelist, make full proof of thy ministry." Our response to the culture rejecting biblical doctrines and seeking to create a culture void of Godly influence is to do the work of an evangelist. Reaching people with the Gospel allows for the work of the Holy Spirit to change hearts and minds, bringing them into agreement with God's word without passing any laws.

It is easy for individuals and church groups to take a political stand on issues of morality—to vote for referendums, support political candidates and civil laws that attempt to change the culture. It takes faith, commitment, and self-sacrifice to become an evangelist for the Gospel, and many of the Christian community are not willing to confront the culture with the Gospel.

Christians and Church groups are willing to experience personal sacrifice in time, money and persecution to promote civil change through the political system, but will not engage their family, neighbors and community with the Gospel. This is an ego-centric position to take, to enforce behavior of others to have a civil environment that reflects a Christian world view in the place of the Holy Spirit changing hearts and minds that lead to not only changes of behavior but brings a lost soul in fellowship with the Creator.

The moral teachings based on the Judeo-Christian theology espoused by our founders and reflected in the laws of America has been rejected by the majority of Americans. The laws drafted and approved by our government that made illegal many of the behaviors the Christian community defined as sins have been for decades under attack by the secular movement. Laws defining legal and illegal acts of sexual behavior have been re-written as our culture becomes more Godless.

As America becomes less populated by Christians, the institutions controlled by the government reflect this shift in the paradigm with changing laws and policies to reflect the culture in America.

With the same determination, the church's institutions exercised to socially engineer a civil legal structure to promote Christian values and behavior. The social progressive movement has employed the same political tactics used by the church's institutions to change the political structure to reflect their values and behavior.

The culture of America has, is, and will change, and given the nature of our governmental structure the laws have been and will continue to reflect the culture of America. The solution for the Lord's church in the Post-Christian era is simple, *do the work of an evangelist.* The Lord's Church is alive and is not damaged by the cultural changes in America, the churches' institutions however are going to suffer great loss if they do not abandon biblical teachings. Christians in the Post-Christian Era are going to be forced to decide if they are willing to abandon church institutions espousing the current cultural acceptance of morality, or if they will abandon the teachings of the Apostles. God's people are encouraged to "choose you this day whom ye will serve." If your church has not espoused the current culture, be assured if it continues to be accepted in the fabric of the American culture it will; *decide now who you will serve.*

THE CONCLUSION OF THE WHOLE MATTER

As this book is penned, Mr. Obama is in office as President of the United States. He has on numerous occasions suggested that America is no longer a Christian nation. The most noted statement made was delivered as a part of a speech in his key-note address to a "Call to Renewal" conference sponsored by the progressive Christian magazine *Sojourners*. In this speech, Obama said, "Whatever we once were, we are no longer a Christian nation – at least, not just. We are also a Jewish nation, a Muslim nation, a Buddhist nation, and a Hindu nation, and a nation of nonbelievers."

President Obama came under extreme criticism by many of the Christian institutions for this statement, "we are no longer a Christian nation." Truly though, we must ask ourselves, *Was Obama speaking truth in this statement?* We have already concluded America was formed independent of a national religion. The in-fluence of Judeo-Christianity was the basis for much of the in-fluence in the formation of her controlling documents, but there was no intent of the founding fathers to establish a national reli-gion, in fact, quite the opposite is true. The founding documents of America precludes the establishment of a national religion, but at the same time forbids the civil government from hindering citizens from practicing religious activities.

In the days ahead, church groups that hold to biblical teach-ings of the sinful nature of homosexual activities will be public-ly shamed and politically punished for their biblical teachings. Many church groups have responded to the issue of homosexual behavior in the same way much of Christendom responded to the sexual revolution of the sixties, to remain silent so as not to effect the attendance in the institution of the church. These groups claim teaching the truth on sexual deviancy sequesters the sinner from God's love and God's love overshadows biblical teachings.

The church institutions embracing the normalcy of sexual deviants will survive and even prosper in the Post-Christian Era, but at the cost of God's removal of His blessings and His Holy Spirit. These Church groups will operate outside biblical teachings and will be focused on institutional ideology.

America has been moving towards an anti-Christian political structure for decades. Flying the flag of civil rights and individual freedoms, godless forces have been doing the bidding of Satan to establish sinful behaviors. The intent of these groups is to establish sexual deviancy as not just normal but impose these behaviors on people and institutions resisting involvement and approval of the sexual deviancy of a small minority of less than three percent of the American population.

God's plan for His people was never to establish their lives of worship in the cultures of the nations, but rather God's call is to, "Come out from among them." Jesus' statement, "when the Son of man cometh, shall he find faith on the earth?" rings true of the American Church in the Post-Christian Era.